JOHN
MACARTHUR

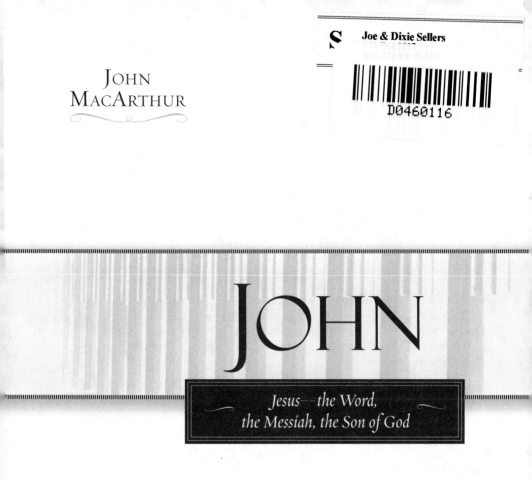

JOHN

*Jesus—the Word,
the Messiah, the Son of God*

THOMAS NELSON
Since 1798

NASHVILLE   DALLAS   MEXICO CITY   RIO DE JANEIRO   BEIJING

JOHN
MACARTHUR BIBLE STUDIES

Published in Nashville, Tennessee. Thomas Nelson is a trademark of Thomas Nelson, Inc.

Thomas Nelson, Inc. titles may be purchased in bulk for education, business, fundraising, or sales promotional use. For information, please email SpecialMarkets@ThomasNelson.com.

Published in association with the literary agency of Wolgemuth & Associates, Inc.

Produced with the assistance of the Livingstone Corporation. Project staff include Jake Barton, Betsy Todt Schmitt, and Andy Culbertson. Project editors: Mary Horner Collins, Amber Rae, and Len Woods

Cover Art by Kirk Luttrell, Livingstone Corporation
Interior Design and Composition by Joel Bartlett, Livingstone Corporation

ISBN-10: 1-4185-0873-X
ISBN-13: 978-1-4185-0873-9

Printed in the United States of America.

08 09 10 RRD 10 9 8

CONTENTS

Introduction to John

The title of the fourth Gospel was identified originally as "According to John." Like the others, "The Gospel" was added later.

Author and Date

Although the author's name does not appear in the Gospel, early church tradition strongly and consistently identified him as the apostle John. The early church father Irenaeus (AD 130–200) was a disciple of Polycarp (AD 70–160), a disciple of the apostle John, and he testified on Polycarp's authority that John had written the Gospel during his residence at Ephesus in Asia Minor when he was advanced in age (*Against Heresies* 2.22.5; 3.1.1). Subsequent to Irenaeus, all the church fathers assumed John to be the Gospel's author. Clement of Alexandria (AD 150–215) wrote that John, aware of the facts set forth in the other Gospels and being moved by the Holy Spirit, composed a "spiritual Gospel" (see Eusebius's *Ecclesiastical History* 6.14.7).

Significant internal characteristics of the book reinforce these early church traditions. While the Synoptic Gospels (Matthew, Mark, Luke) identify the apostle John by name approximately twenty times (including parallels), he is not directly mentioned by name in the Gospel of John. Instead, the author prefers to identify himself as the disciple "whom Jesus loved" (13:23; 19:26; 20:2; 21:7, 20). The absence of any mention of John's name directly is remarkable when one considers the important part played by other named disciples in this Gospel. Yet, the recurring designation of himself as the disciple "whom Jesus loved," a deliberate avoidance by John of his personal name, reflects his humility and celebrates his relation to the Lord Jesus. No mention of John's name was necessary because the original readers clearly understood that he was the Gospel's author. Also, through a process of elimination based primarily on analyzing the material in chapters 20 and 21, this disciple "whom Jesus loved" narrows down to the apostle John (for example, 21:2, 24). The Gospel's author is exacting in mentioning the names of other characters in the book; thus, if the author had been someone other than John the apostle, he would not have omitted John's name.

The Gospel's anonymity strongly reinforces the arguments favoring John's authorship, for only someone of his well-known and preeminent authority as an apostle would have been able to write a Gospel that differed so markedly in form and substance from the other Gospels and have it receive unanimous acceptance

1

in the early church. In contrast, apocryphal Gospels produced from the mid-second century onward, and falsely ascribed to apostles or other famous persons closely associated with Jesus, were universally rejected by the church.

John and James, his older brother (Acts 12:2), were known as "the sons of Zebedee" (Matt. 10:2–4), and Jesus called them "Sons of Thunder" (Mark 3:17). John was an apostle (Luke 6:12–16) and one of the three most intimate associates of Jesus (along with Peter and James—see Matthew 17:1; 26:37), being an eyewitness to and participant in Jesus' earthly ministry (1 John 1:1–4). After Christ's ascension, John became a pillar in the Jerusalem church (Gal. 2:9). He ministered with Peter (Acts 3:1; 4:13; 8:14) until he went to Ephesus (tradition says before the destruction of Jerusalem), from where he wrote this Gospel and from where the Romans exiled him to Patmos (Rev. 1:9). Besides the Gospel that bears his name, John also authored 1 John, 2 John, 3 John, and Revelation (Rev. 1:1).

Because the writings of some church fathers indicate that John was actively writing in his old age and that he was already aware of the Synoptic Gospels, many date the Gospel sometime after the synoptics' composition, but prior to John's writing of 1 John, 2 John, 3 John, and Revelation. John wrote his Gospel around AD 80–90, about fifty years after witnessing Jesus' earthly ministry.

BACKGROUND AND SETTING

Strategic to John's background and setting is the fact that, according to tradition, John was aware of the Synoptic Gospels. Apparently, he wrote his Gospel in order to make a unique contribution to the record of the Lord's life (a spiritual Gospel) and, in part, to be supplementary as well as complementary to Matthew, Mark, and Luke. The Gospel's unique characteristics reinforce this purpose.

First, John supplied a large amount of unique material not recorded in the other Gospels. Second, he often supplied information that helps the understanding of the events in the Synoptics. For example, while the Synoptics begin with Jesus' ministry in Galilee, they imply that Jesus had a ministry prior to that (for example, Matt. 4:12; Mark 1:14). John supplies the answer with information on Jesus' prior ministry in Judea (chapter 3) and Samaria (chapter 4). In Mark 6:45, after the feeding of the five thousand, Jesus compelled His disciples to cross the Sea of Galilee to Bethsaida. John recorded the reason: The people were about to make Jesus king because of His miraculous multiplying of food, and He was avoiding their ill-motivated efforts (John 6:26).

Third, John is the most theological of the Gospels, containing, for example, a heavily theological prologue (1:1–18), larger amounts of didactic and discourse material in proportion to narrative (for example, 3:13–17), and the largest amount of teaching on the Holy Spirit (for example, 14:16–17, 26; 16:7–14). Although

2

John was aware of the Synoptics and fashioned his Gospel with them in mind, he did not depend upon them for information. Rather, under the inspiration of the Holy Spirit, he utilized his own memory as an eyewitness in composing the Gospel (1:14; 19:35; 21:24). John's Gospel is the only one of the four to contain a precise statement regarding the author's purpose (20:30–31). He declares, "These are written that you may believe that Jesus is the Christ, the Son of God, and that believing you may have life in His name" (20:31). Thus John had two primary purposes: evangelistic and apologetic. Reinforcing the evangelistic purpose is the fact that the word "believe" occurs approximately one hundred times in the Gospel (the Synoptics use the term less than half as much). John composed his Gospel to provide reasons for saving faith and, as a result, to assure readers that they would receive the divine gift of eternal life (1:12).

The apologetic purpose is closely related to the evangelistic purpose. John wrote to convince his readers of Jesus' true identity as the incarnate God-man whose divine and human natures were perfectly united into one person who was the prophesied Christ ("Messiah") and Savior of the world (for example, 1:41; 3:16; 4:25–26; 8:58). He organized his whole Gospel around eight "signs," or proofs that reinforce Jesus' true identity, leading to faith. The first half of his work revolves around seven miraculous signs selected to reveal Christ's person and engender belief: (1) turning water into wine (2:1–11); (2) healing the royal official's son (4:46–54); (3) healing the lame man (5:1–18); (4) feeding the multitude (6:1–15); (5) walking on water (6:16–21); (6) healing the blind man (9:1–41); and (7) raising Lazarus from the dead (11:1–57). The eighth sign is the miraculous catch of fish (21:6–11) after Jesus' resurrection.

HISTORICAL AND THEOLOGICAL THEMES

In accordance with John's evangelistic and apologetic purposes, the overall message of the Gospel is found in 20:31: "Jesus is the Christ, the Son of God." The book, therefore, centers on the person and work of Christ. Three predominant words—"signs," "believe," and "life"—in 20:30–31 receive constant emphasis throughout the Gospel to enforce the theme of salvation in Christ, which is first set forth in the prologue (1:1–18; see also 1 John 1:1–4) and expressed throughout the Gospel in varying ways (for example, 6:35, 48; 8:12; 10:7, 9, 11–14; 11:25; 14:6; 17:3). In addition, John provides the record of how men responded to Jesus Christ and the salvation that He offered. Summing up, John's Gospel focuses on: (1) Jesus as the Word, the Messiah, and Son of God; (2) Who brings the gift of salvation to people; (3) who either accept or reject the offer.

John also presents certain contrastive sub-themes that reinforce his main theme. He uses dualism (life and death, light and darkness, love and hate, from above and from below) to convey vital information about the person and work of Christ and the need to believe in Him (for example, 1:4–5, 12–13; 3:16–21; 12:44–46; 15:17–20).

John also includes seven emphatic "I am" statements that identify Jesus as God and Messiah (6:35; 8:12; 10:7, 9, 11, 14; 11:25; 14:6; 15:1, 5).

INTERPRETIVE CHALLENGES

Because John composed his record in a clear and simple style, one might tend to underestimate the depth of this Gospel. Since John's Gospel is a "spiritual" Gospel, the truths he conveys are profound. The reader must prayerfully and meticulously explore the book in order to discover the vast richness of the spiritual treasures that the apostle, under the guidance of the Holy Spirit (14:26; 16:13), has lovingly deposited in his Gospel.

THE INCARNATION OF THE SON OF GOD

DRAWING NEAR

Many opinions abound about who Jesus is. What are some of the more common ideas about the identity of Jesus held today that come to mind?

_____

_____

_____

Who do you believe Jesus is? Why?

_____

_____

_____

THE CONTEXT

This rich theological passage constitutes what is known as the prologue to John's Gospel. It introduces many of the major themes that John will address, especially the main theme that "Jesus is the Christ, the Son of God" (vv. 12–14; cf. 20:31). Several key words repeated throughout the Gospel (for example, _life, light, witness, glory_) appear here for the first time. The remainder of the Gospel develops the theme of the prologue as to how the eternal "Word" of God, Jesus the Messiah and Son of God, became flesh and ministered among people so that all who believe in Him would be saved.

Although John wrote the prologue with the simplest vocabulary in the New Testament, the truths that the prologue conveys are the most profound. The prologue features six basic truths about Christ as the Son of God:

- The eternal Christ (vv. 1–3)
- The incarnate Christ (vv. 4–5)
- The forerunner of Christ (vv. 6–8)
- The unrecognized Christ (vv. 9–11)—that is, His rejection
- The omnipotent Christ (vv. 12–13)
- The glorious Christ (vv. 14–18)—that is, His deity

As you begin, ask God to open the spiritual eyes of your heart to the truth He wants you to see in this lesson.

KEYS TO THE TEXT

Incarnation: A theological term for the coming of God's Son into the world as a human being. The term itself is not used in the Bible, but it is based on clear references in the New Testament to Jesus as a person "in the flesh." The Greek construction of the term "the Word" used in the Gospel of John emphasizes that the Word had all the essence or attributes of deity, i.e., Jesus the Messiah was fully God. Although in His incarnation Christ became fully man, He took only the outward appearance of sinful flesh, because He was completely without sin (Heb. 4:15). To know Jesus is to know God. This constant emphasis on Jesus as God incarnate is unmistakably clear in this Gospel.

Life, Light, Darkness: John introduces the reader to contrasting themes that occur throughout the Gospel. "Life" and "light" are qualities of the Word that are shared not only among the Godhead, but also by those who respond to the gospel message regarding Jesus Christ. John uses the word "life" about thirty-six times in his Gospel, far more than any other New Testament book. It refers not only in a broad sense to physical and temporal life that the Son imparted to the created world as the agent of creation, but especially to spiritual and eternal life imparted as a gift through belief in Him.

In Scripture, "light" and "darkness" are familiar symbols. John uses the term "darkness" fourteen times (eight in the Gospel and six in 1 John) out of its seventeen occurrences in the New Testament, making it almost an exclusive Johannine word. Intellectually, light refers to biblical truth while darkness refers to error or falsehood. Morally, light refers to holiness or purity while darkness refers to sin or wrongdoing.

UNLEASHING THE TEXT

Read 1:1–18, noting the key words and definitions next to the passage.

in the beginning (v. 1)—In an absolute sense, this phrase refers to the beginning of the space-time universe.

the Word (v. 1)—The Greek term is *logos*, and in extrabiblical, philosophical literature it stood for impersonal wisdom, rational principle, or divine

John 1:1–18 (NKJV)

1 *In the beginning was the Word, and the Word was with God, and the Word was God.*

2 *He was in the beginning with God.*

3 *All things were made through Him, and without Him nothing was made that was made.*

4 *In Him was life, and the life was the light of men.*

5 *And the light shines in the darkness, and the darkness did not comprehend it.*

6 *There was a man sent from God, whose name was John.*

7 *This man came for a witness, to bear witness of the Light, that all through him might believe.*

8 *He was not that Light, but was sent to bear witness of that Light.*

9 *That was the true Light which gives light to every man coming into the world.*

10 *He was in the world, and the world was made through Him, and the world did not know Him.*

11 *He came to His own, and His own did not receive Him.*

12 *But as many as received Him, to them He gave the right to become children of God, to those who believe in His name:*

13 *who were born, not of blood, nor of the will of the flesh, nor of the will of man, but of God.*

14 *And the Word became flesh and dwelt among us, and we beheld His glory, the glory as of the only begotten of the Father, full of grace and truth.*

15 *John bore witness of Him and cried out, saying, "This was He of whom I said, 'He who comes after me is preferred before me, for He was before me.'"*

16 *And of His fullness we have all received, and grace for grace.*

17 *For the law was given through Moses, but grace and truth came through Jesus Christ.*

18 *No one has seen God at any time. The only begotten Son, who is in the bosom of the Father, He has declared Him.*

reason; here John imbued the concept with personality.

the Word was with God (v. 1)—The Word, as the Second Person of the Trinity, was in intimate fellowship with God the Father throughout all eternity.

the Word was God (v. 1)—The Word had all the essence or attributes of deity; that is, Jesus the Messiah was (and is) fully God.

all things were made through Him (v. 3)—Jesus Christ was God the Father's agent in creation.

the true Light . . . coming into the world (v. 9)—better rendered "the true Light which, coming into the world, gives light to every man"

His own . . . His own (v. 11)—in the first case, a reference to humanity in general; in the latter instance, a reference to the Jewish nation

as many as received Him . . . to those who believe in His name (v. 12)—To receive Him who is the Word of God means to acknowledge His claims, place one's faith in Him, and thereby yield allegiance to Him.

the Word became flesh (v. 14)—The word "became" emphasizes the eternal, uncreated Christ taking on humanity at a specific point in space-time history.

dwelt (v. 14)—literally, "pitched a tabernacle/tent"; a reference to the Old Testament tabernacle where God met with Israel before the temple was built

1) What descriptions (titles and terms) does John use to introduce the person of Jesus Christ?

2) What was John the Baptist's role? Why is he significant?

_____

_____

_____

3) According to John, how was the arrival of Christ into the New Testament world different from the coming of the law into the Old Testament world?

_____

_____

_____

(Verses to consider: Rom. 3:19–20; Gal. 3:10–14)

GOING DEEPER

To gain a fuller picture of the uniqueness and deity of Christ, read the related passage of Colossians 1:13–20.

EXPLORING THE MEANING

4) What does the Bible mean when it refers to *darkness*? To *light*?

_____

_____

_____

_____

(Verses to consider: Ps. 119:105; Prov. 6:23; Rom. 13:11–14; 1 Thess. 5:4–7; 1 John 1:5–7)

5) What is significant about the fact that Christ is the source of light and life (v. 4)?

_____

_____

_____

_____

(Verses to consider: John 8:12; 9:5; 10:28; 11:25–26; 14:6)

6) What profound truth is expressed in John 1:14? What are the implications of this for your life?

_____

_____

_____

(Verses to consider: Exod. 25:8; 33:7, 11)

TRUTH FOR TODAY

There have been many false views of Jesus throughout history, from noble example to political revolutionary. Yet to imagine a Jesus who was not the Savior is as foolish as to imagine a Shakespeare who was not a writer, or a Rembrandt who was not a painter. His name is *Jesus,* not because He is our example, guide, leader, or friend, though He is all of those things. His name is Jesus because He is our *Savior.*

REFLECTING ON THE TEXT

C. S. Lewis wrote: "I am trying here to prevent anyone saying the really foolish thing that people often say about [Christ]: 'I'm ready to accept Jesus as a great moral teacher, but I don't accept His claim to be God.' That is the one thing we must not say. A man who was merely a man and said the sort of things Jesus said would not be a great moral teacher. He would either be a lunatic—on a level with the man who says he is a poached egg—or else he would be the Devil of Hell. You must make your choice. Either this man was, and is, the Son of God: or else a madman or something worse. You can shut Him up for a fool; you can spit at Him and kill Him as a demon; or you can fall at His feet and call Him Lord and God. But let us not come up with any patronizing nonsense about His being a great moral teacher. He has not left that open to us. He did not intend to." (*Mere Christianity,* New York: Macmillan Publishing Company, 1960, pp. 40–41)

7) Based on John's prologue, how would you answer the person who claimed that Jesus was just a good man or a wise teacher?

_____

_____

_____

_____

8) Describe the time in your life when you "received" Christ, or believed in His name.

Age 18, Birth of my Son 2½ moms. Early. Doctors pronuced him dead.

9) Which of your friends and neighbors need to know the grace and truth that come only through Jesus Christ? Pray for these friends this week.

Most of them,

PERSONAL RESPONSE

Write out additional reflections, questions you may have, or a prayer.

Our Heavenly Father, please please hold my heart & my eyes on Jesus my Savior the Light - Let my actions always speak Louder of you then anything. Let me always be a g

The Presentation of the Son of God

John 1:19–2:25

Drawing Near

What aspects of Jesus' identity mean the most to you right now? Why?

_____

_____

_____

What aspects of Jesus' identity do you have questions about?

_____

_____

_____

Ask God to give you deeper insight into Jesus' identity as you begin this study.

_____

_____

_____

The Context

Following his deeply theological prologue, John introduces the first of many witnesses to prove that Jesus is the Messiah and Son of God. This is the main theme of his Gospel (20:31). First we see John the Baptist giving testimony on three different days to three different audiences. These events took place in AD 26–27, just a few months after John's baptism of Jesus. Next we find the record of Jesus' first public miracle—changing water into wine at a wedding in Cana of Galilee. This astounding sign was another powerful witness (the first of eight confirming miracles chosen by John) that pointed unmistakably to Jesus' deity. Finally, John's account of Jesus cleansing the temple in righteous indignation was added proof of Christ's deity and messiahship. The incident demonstrated Jesus' passion for God's house to be honored and His promised power of resurrection.

KEYS TO THE TEXT

Son of God: There are two basic events in relation to which Jesus Christ is Son— His virgin birth and His resurrection. He was not a son until He was born into this world through the virgin birth. In describing one of the predictions of this birth, Luke says, "And the angel answered and said to her, 'The Holy Spirit will come upon you, and the power of the Most High will overshadow you; and for that reason the holy offspring shall be called the Son of God' " (Luke 1:35 NKJV). The sonship of Christ is inextricably connected with His incarnation. Only after Christ's incarnation did God say, "This is My Son" (Luke 3:22 NKJV).

His sonship came to full bloom in His resurrection. This deep truth Paul makes clear in the book of Romans: "Concerning His Son, who was born of a descendant of David according to the flesh, who was declared the Son of God with power by the resurrection from the dead, according to the spirit of holiness, Jesus Christ our Lord" (Rom. 1:3–4 NJKV). He became a Son at birth; He was declared to be a Son in resurrection.

Messiah: The one anointed by God and empowered by God's Spirit to deliver His people and establish His kingdom. In Jewish thought, the Messiah would be the king of the Jews, a political leader who would defeat their enemies and bring in a golden era of peace and prosperity. In Christian thought, the term *Messiah* refers to Jesus' role as a spiritual deliverer, setting His people free from sin and death. The word *Messiah* comes from a Hebrew term that means "anointed one." Its Greek counterpart is *Christos,* from which the word *Christ* comes. (*Nelson's New Illustrated Bible Dictionary*)

UNLEASHING THE TEXT

Read 1:19–2:25, noting the key words and definitions next to the passage.

John 1:19–2:25 (NKJV)

19 *Now this is the testimony of John, when the Jews sent priests and Levites from Jerusalem to ask him, "Who are you?"*

Christ (v. 20)—The term is the Greek equivalent of the Hebrew term for "Messiah."

20 *He confessed, and did not deny, but confessed, "I am not the Christ."*

"Are you Elijah?" (v. 21)—Malachi 4:5 promises the return of the prophet Elijah before the coming of Messiah to establish His earthly kingdom. Luke 1:17 clarifies that this role could have been fulfilled by someone other than the literal, historical Elijah.

21 *And they asked him, "What then? Are you Elijah?" He said, "I am not." "Are you the Prophet?" And he answered, "No."*

22 *Then they said to him, "Who are you, that we may give an answer to those who sent us? What do you say about yourself?"*

23 He said: "I am 'The voice of one crying in the wilderness: "Make straight the way of the Lord," ' as the prophet Isaiah said."

24 Now those who were sent were from the Pharisees.

25 And they asked him, saying, "Why then do you baptize if you are not the Christ, nor Elijah, nor the Prophet?"

26 John answered them, saying, "I baptize with water, but there stands One among you whom you do not know.

27 It is He who, coming after me, is preferred before me, whose sandal strap I am not worthy to loose."

28 These things were done in Bethabara beyond the Jordan, where John was baptizing.

29 The next day John saw Jesus coming toward him, and said, "Behold! The Lamb of God who takes away the sin of the world!

30 This is He of whom I said, 'After me comes a Man who is preferred before me, for He was before me.'

31 I did not know Him; but that He should be revealed to Israel, therefore I came baptizing with water."

32 And John bore witness, saying, "I saw the Spirit descending from heaven like a dove, and He remained upon Him.

33 I did not know Him, but He who sent me to baptize with water said to me, 'Upon whom you see the Spirit descending, and remaining on Him, this is He who baptizes with the Holy Spirit.'

34 And I have seen and testified that this is the Son of God."

35 Again, the next day, John stood with two of his disciples.

36 And looking at Jesus as He walked, he said, "Behold the Lamb of God!"

37 The two disciples heard him speak, and they followed Jesus.

38 Then Jesus turned, and seeing them following, said to them, "What do you seek?" They said to Him, "Rabbi" (which is to say, when translated, Teacher), "where are You staying?"

"Are you the Prophet?" (v. 21)— This refers to Deuteronomy 18:15–18, which most interpreted as referring to a forerunner of Messiah, but which the New Testament applies to Christ Himself.

the Lamb of God (v. 29)—A lamb was used by the Jews during Passover for sacrificial purposes; here John applies the expression to the ultimate sacrifice of Jesus on the cross to atone for the sins of the world.

sin of the world (v. 29)—Jesus' sacrifice for sin is offered to all human beings without distinction.

the Son of God (v. 34)—a reference to the unique oneness and intimacy that Jesus sustains to the Father as "Son"

they followed Jesus (v. 37)—The implication is that they went after Jesus to examine Him more closely because of John's testimony.

13

the tenth hour (v. 39)—4 PM since the Jews considered 6 AM as the start of a new day

Messiah (v. 41)—literally, "Anointed One," the deliverer promised in the Old Testament who would be prophet, priest, and king of God's people

Cephas (v. 42)—Aramaic for "rock," which translates to "Peter" in Greek

"Can anything good come out of Nazareth?" (v. 46)—Nazareth was an insignificant village without seeming to have any prophetic significance.

no deceit (v. 47)—The idea is that he had an honest, seeking heart.

I saw you (v. 48)—a reference to Christ's supernatural knowledge

Son of Man (v. 51)—Jesus' favorite self-designation; it alludes to Daniel 7:13–14 and thus refers to the coming of the Messiah and His kingdom

39 He said to them, "Come and see." They came and saw where He was staying, and remained with Him that day (now it was about the tenth hour).

40 One of the two who heard John speak, and followed Him, was Andrew, Simon Peter's brother.

41 He first found his own brother Simon, and said to him, "We have found the Messiah" (which is translated, the Christ).

42 And he brought him to Jesus. Now when Jesus looked at him, He said, "You are Simon the son of Jonah. You shall be called Cephas" (which is translated, A Stone).

43 The following day Jesus wanted to go to Galilee, and He found Philip and said to him, "Follow Me."

44 Now Philip was from Bethsaida, the city of Andrew and Peter.

45 Philip found Nathanael and said to him, "We have found Him of whom Moses in the law, and also the prophets, wrote—Jesus of Nazareth, the son of Joseph."

46 And Nathanael said to him, "Can anything good come out of Nazareth?" Philip said to him, "Come and see."

47 Jesus saw Nathanael coming toward Him, and said of him, "Behold, an Israelite indeed, in whom is no deceit!"

48 Nathanael said to Him, "How do You know me?" Jesus answered and said to him, "Before Philip called you, when you were under the fig tree, I saw you."

49 Nathanael answered and said to Him, "Rabbi, You are the Son of God! You are the King of Israel!"

50 Jesus answered and said to him, "Because I said to you, 'I saw you under the fig tree,' do you believe? You will see greater things than these."

51 And He said to him, "Most assuredly, I say to you, hereafter you shall see heaven open, and the angels of God ascending and descending upon the Son of Man."

2:1 On the third day there was a wedding in Cana of Galilee, and the mother of Jesus was there.

2 *Now both Jesus and His disciples were invited to the wedding.*

3 *And when they ran out of wine, the mother of Jesus said to Him, "They have no wine."*

4 *Jesus said to her, "Woman, what does your concern have to do with Me? My hour has not yet come."*

5 *His mother said to the servants, "Whatever He says to you, do it."*

6 *Now there were set there six waterpots of stone, according to the manner of purification of the Jews, containing twenty or thirty gallons apiece.*

7 *Jesus said to them, "Fill the waterpots with water." And they filled them up to the brim.*

8 *And He said to them, "Draw some out now, and take it to the master of the feast." And they took it.*

9 *When the master of the feast had tasted the water that was made wine, and did not know where it came from (but the servants who had drawn the water knew), the master of the feast called the bridegroom.*

10 *And he said to him, "Every man at the beginning sets out the good wine, and when the guests have well drunk, then the inferior. You have kept the good wine until now!"*

11 *This beginning of signs Jesus did in Cana of Galilee, and manifested His glory; and His disciples believed in Him.*

12 *After this He went down to Capernaum, He, His mother, His brothers, and His disciples; and they did not stay there many days.*

13 *Now the Passover of the Jews was at hand, and Jesus went up to Jerusalem.*

14 *And He found in the temple those who sold oxen and sheep and doves, and the money changers doing business.*

15 *When He had made a whip of cords, He drove them all out of the temple, with the sheep and the oxen, and poured out the changers' money and overturned the tables.*

Woman (2:4)—Not impolite, but a formal way of distancing Jesus from His mother; perhaps the idea is "ma'am."

My hour has not yet come (v. 4)—The phrase refers to Jesus' death and exaltation; the idea may be that the cross must come before the blessings of the millennial age can be poured out.

signs (v. 11)—significant displays of power that point to deeper divine realities

Jesus went up to Jerusalem (v. 13)—standard practice for every devout Jewish male over twelve years of age

do not make (v. 15)—literally "stop making;" a call for the cessation of their money-grubbing practices

the Jews (v. 18)—most likely the temple authorities and members of the Sanhedrin

16 And He said to those who sold doves, "Take these things away! Do not make My Father's house a house of merchandise!"

17 Then His disciples remembered that it was written, "Zeal for Your house has eaten Me up."

18 So the Jews answered and said to Him, "What sign do You show to us, since You do these things?"

19 Jesus answered and said to them, "Destroy this temple, and in three days I will raise it up."

20 Then the Jews said, "It has taken forty-six years to build this temple, and will You raise it up in three days?"

21 But He was speaking of the temple of His body.

22 Therefore, when He had risen from the dead, His disciples remembered that He had said this to them; and they believed the Scripture and the word which Jesus had said.

23 Now when He was in Jerusalem at the Passover, during the feast, many believed in His name when they saw the signs which He did.

24 But Jesus did not commit Himself to them, because He knew all men,

25 and had no need that anyone should testify of man, for He knew what was in man.

1) In what ways were the Jews confused by the appearance of John the Baptist?

_____

_____

_____

2) What insights into John the Baptist's character does this passage reveal? Describe his personality.

_____

_____

_____

_____

3) What was Philip's assessment of Jesus? Why is this significant?

_____

_____

_____

(Verses to consider: Deut. 18:15–19; Luke 24:44, 47; Acts 10:43; 18:28; 26:22–23; Rom. 1:2; 1 Cor. 15:3–4)

GOING DEEPER

The Old Testament often illuminates events in the New Testament. Read Exodus 12:1–14 for more understanding of the Jewish Passover.

EXPLORING THE MEANING

4) How does Jesus Christ fit John's description as the "lamb of God"? How does His sacrifice parallel the Old Testament Passover?

_____

_____

_____

_____

5) What did Christ reveal about Himself in the miracle at the wedding in Cana of Galilee?

His 1st _____

_____

_____

_____

6) Why did Jesus react with such anger as He cleared the temple? What was the purpose?

_____

_____

_____

(Verses to consider: Ps. 69:9; Mal. 3:1–3)

Truth for Today

If Jesus had been the military Messiah the people wanted, He would have brought an army into Jerusalem and attacked the main Roman garrison at Fort Antonius. Instead, alone and weaponless, He attacked a group of His fellow countrymen who were profaning the temple. The supreme issue for Jesus was not Rome's army but God's temple. The Messiah did not come as a military, economic, political, or social savior from injustice and oppression, but as a spiritual Savior from sin and death. At His Second Coming He will indeed make right the injustices and inequities that plague mankind. But before He comes again as King of kings and Lord of lords to establish His glorious millennial kingdom and to resolve all the conflicts of fallen mankind, He first had to come as Savior to establish His spiritual kingdom within those who trust Him.

Reflecting on the Text

7) From these first glimpses of Jesus in action in John 1–2, what would you say was Jesus' main agenda?

Salvation

8) Christ became angry with those who demonstrated irreverence and who impeded the worship of others. As you reflect on your own habits of worship, what are some ways you personally can treat God's house with more reverence? How can your church congregation demonstrate greater reverence for God?

9) What qualities from the life of John the Baptist do you want to emulate? Why?

10) This passage depicts both true, devoted followers of Christ and others who seemed to be marked by only a superficial enthusiasm for Christ. Which are you more like on most days? Why? What do you need to change?

devoted - Get into

PERSONAL RESPONSE

Write out additional reflections, questions you may have, or a prayer.

ADDITIONAL NOTES

3
YOU MUST BE BORN AGAIN!

DRAWING NEAR

If you could go back in history and have a private conversation with Jesus, what is one question you would ask? Why?

_____

_____

_____

THE CONTEXT

The beloved and familiar story of Jesus' nighttime encounter with Nicodemus reinforces John's overarching themes that Jesus is the Messiah and Son of God and that He came to offer salvation to people. The former might be described as John's apologetic purpose—the latter, his evangelistic purpose. In gently confronting Nicodemus with his need for regeneration, Jesus demonstrated His identity as God's messenger.

The chapter may be divided into three sections: (1) Jesus' dialogue with Nicodemus; (2) Jesus' discourse on God's plan of salvation; (3) John the Baptist's last testimony regarding Christ.

As John's ministry faded, Jesus' ministry moved to the forefront. Despite the fact that John the Baptist received widespread fame in Israel and was generally accepted by the common people of the land as well as by those who were social outcasts, his testimony regarding Jesus was rejected, especially by the leaders of Israel.

This is a rich passage, brimming with practical truth for modern men and women.

KEYS TO THE TEXT

Born Again: The phrase literally means "born from above." It refers to the very core of the human problem, i.e., the need for spiritual transformation or regeneration produced by the Holy Spirit. New birth is an act of God whereby eternal life is imparted to the believer (2 Cor. 5:17; Titus 3:5; 1 Pet. 1:3; 1 John 2:29; 3:9; 4:7; 5:1, 4, 18). John 1:12–13 indicates that being born again also carries the idea "to become children of God." The new birth must be appropriated by an act of faith.

Eternal Life: There are ten references in John's Gospel to "eternal life." The same Greek word is translated eight times as "everlasting life." The two expressions appear in the New Testament nearly fifty times. Eternal life refers not only to eternal quantity but also divine quality of life. It means literally, "life of the age to come," and refers therefore to resurrection and heavenly existence in perfect glory and holiness. This life for believers in the Lord Jesus is experienced before heaven is reached. This "eternal life" is in essence nothing less than participation in the eternal life of the Living Word, Jesus Christ. It is the life of God in every believer, yet not fully manifest until the resurrection (Rom. 8:19–23; Phil. 3:20, 21).

UNLEASHING THE TEXT

Read 3:1–36, noting the key words and definitions next to the passage.

John 3:1–36 (NKJV)

Pharisees (v. 1)—The name possibly derives from a Hebrew word meaning "to separate." These leaders were highly zealous for ritual and religious purity according to both the Mosaic law and their own traditions.

a ruler of the Jews (v. 1)—a reference to his membership in the Sanhedrin, the main ruling body of the Jews in Palestine; a kind of supreme court

came to Jesus by night (v. 2)—likely because he was afraid to been seen openly associating with the controversial Jesus

born of water and the Spirit (v. 5)—not literal water, but an allusion to Old Testament imagery and the need for cleansing and purification

the wind blows where it wishes (v. 8)—The Spirit, like the wind, cannot be controlled or understood; however, its effects can be seen.

1 *There was a man of the Pharisees named Nicodemus, a ruler of the Jews.*

2 *This man came to Jesus by night and said to Him, "Rabbi, we know that You are a teacher come from God; for no one can do these signs that You do unless God is with him."*

3 *Jesus answered and said to him, "Most assuredly, I say to you, unless one is born again, he cannot see the kingdom of God."*

4 *Nicodemus said to Him, "How can a man be born when he is old? Can he enter a second time into his mother's womb and be born?"*

5 *Jesus answered, "Most assuredly, I say to you, unless one is born of water and the Spirit, he cannot enter the kingdom of God.*

6 *That which is born of the flesh is flesh, and that which is born of the Spirit is spirit.*

7 *Do not marvel that I said to you, 'You must be born again.'*

8 *The wind blows where it wishes, and you hear the sound of it, but cannot tell where it comes from and where it goes. So is everyone who is born of the Spirit."*

9 *Nicodemus answered and said to Him, "How can these things be?"*

10 *Jesus answered and said to him, "Are you the teacher of Israel, and do not know these things?*

11 *Most assuredly, I say to you, We speak what We know and testify what We have seen, and you do not receive Our witness.*

12 *If I have told you earthly things and you do not believe, how will you believe if I tell you heavenly things?*

13 *No one has ascended to heaven but He who came down from heaven, that is, the Son of Man who is in heaven.*

14 *And as Moses lifted up the serpent in the wilderness, even so must the Son of Man be lifted up,*

15 *that whoever believes in Him should not perish but have eternal life.*

16 *For God so loved the world that He gave His only begotten Son, that whoever believes in Him should not perish but have everlasting life.*

17 *For God did not send His Son into the world to condemn the world, but that the world through Him might be saved.*

18 *"He who believes in Him is not condemned; but he who does not believe is condemned already, because he has not believed in the name of the only begotten Son of God.*

19 *And this is the condemnation, that the light has come into the world, and men loved darkness rather than light, because their deeds were evil.*

20 *For everyone practicing evil hates the light and does not come to the light, lest his deeds should be exposed.*

21 *But he who does the truth comes to the light, that his deeds may be clearly seen, that they have been done in God."*

22 *After these things Jesus and His disciples came into the land of Judea, and there He remained with them and baptized.*

23 *Now John also was baptizing in Aenon near Salim, because there was much water there. And they came and were baptized.*

you do not receive our witness (v. 11)—Nicodemus' reluctance to believe the testimony of Jesus and John was typical of the nation's collective doubt.

eternal life (v. 15)—not only eternal in quantity but in quality; the life of God in everyone who believes

believed in the name (v. 18)—More than mere intellectual assent, this refers to trust in and commitment to Christ as Savior and obedience to Him as Lord.

baptized (v. 22)—Jesus' disciples carried on this work, not Jesus Himself (see 4:2).

there arose a dispute (v. 25)—likely in regard to the baptismal practices of Jesus and John vs. the purification rituals of the Jews

24 For John had not yet been thrown into prison.

25 Then there arose a dispute between some of John's disciples and the Jews about purification.

26 And they came to John and said to him, "Rabbi, He who was with you beyond the Jordan, to whom you have testified—behold, He is baptizing, and all are coming to Him!"

given to him from heaven (v. 27)—ministry opportunities are sovereignly bestowed by God

27 John answered and said, "A man can receive nothing unless it has been given to him from heaven.

28 You yourselves bear me witness, that I said, 'I am not the Christ,' but, 'I have been sent before Him.'

bridegroom . . . friend of bridegroom (v. 29)—a parable alluding to Jewish marital practices; a "best man" organized the details and presided over the wedding of his good friend, finding joy in the smooth outworking of the affair

29 He who has the bride is the bridegroom; but the friend of the bridegroom, who stands and hears him, rejoices greatly because of the bridegroom's voice. Therefore this joy of mine is fulfilled.

30 He must increase, but I must decrease.

31 He who comes from above is above all; he who is of the earth is earthly and speaks of the earth. He who comes from heaven is above all.

32 And what He has seen and heard, that He testifies; and no one receives His testimony.

33 He who has received His testimony has certified that God is true.

the Spirit by measure (v. 34)—God gave the Spirit to the Son without limits.

34 For He whom God has sent speaks the words of God, for God does not give the Spirit by measure.

35 The Father loves the Son, and has given all things into His hand.

36 He who believes in the Son has everlasting life; and he who does not believe the Son shall not see life, but the wrath of God abides on him."

1) What facts from Nicodemus' encounter with Jesus lead you to believe that Nicodemus was open to the truth about Jesus?

_____

_____

_____

(Verses to consider: John 7:50–52; 19:38–42)

2) Jesus told Nicodemus, "You must be born again" (or "born from above"). What does this concept mean? How would you explain it in your own words?

_____

_____

_____

_____

3) What was John the Baptist's attitude as Jesus became more prominent and popular? How did John's followers react to these developments?

_____

_____

_____

_____

GOING DEEPER

In the Old Testament, the children of Israel had hard hearts and rebelled against God many times. Read Ezekiel 36:25–28 for what God promised to give them.

EXPLORING THE MEANING

4) How does the message from this Old Testament passage compare with what Jesus said to Nicodemus about the need for regeneration (that is, internal, spiritual transformation)?

_____

_____

_____

_____

5) Read Numbers 21:5–9. Why did Jesus mention this Old Testament event? How does it compare to His own future death?

_____

_____

_____

6) According to John 3, what are the consequences of sincere belief in Jesus (see vv. 12, 13, 16, 18, and 36)?

_____

_____

_____

_____

TRUTH FOR TODAY

A person who is spiritually dead has no life by which he can respond to spiritual things, much less live a spiritual life. No amount of love, care, and words of affection from God can draw a response. A spiritually dead person is alienated from God and therefore alienated from life. He has no capacity to respond. As the great Scottish commentator John Eadie said, "It is a case of death walking." Men apart from God are spiritual zombies, the walking dead who do not know they are dead. They go through the motions of life, but they do not possess it. Above all else, a dead person needs to be made alive. That is what salvation gives—spiritual life. When we became Christians we were no longer alienated from the life of God. We became spiritually alive through union with the death and resurrection of Christ and thereby for the first time became sensitive to God.

REFLECTING ON THE TEXT

7) Describe the events that led to your being "born again." What people or situations or tools did God use?

_____

_____

_____

NOTE: If you are not sure whether you've ever experienced the new birth, turn to God in prayer right now to confess your need for forgiveness, your inability to change yourself, as well as your faith in the fact that Christ alone can forgive sin and impart eternal life. By turning from sin and self and calling on Jesus Christ, you can be saved today! That's the good news!

8) What practical insights into evangelism can you glean from Jesus' encounter with Nicodemus?

_____

_____

_____

_____

9) What attitudes and motives in ministry can you emulate from the life of John the Baptist?

_____

_____

_____

_____

PERSONAL RESPONSE

Write out additional reflections, questions you may have, or a prayer.

_____

_____

_____

_____

_____

_____

_____

_____

_____

_____

ADDITIONAL NOTES

~4~
THE LIVING WATER

DRAWING NEAR

How satisfying is your Christian walk right now? Explain.

_____

_____

In what areas of life do you sense you might be pursuing your own agenda rather than God's will for you?

_____

_____

THE CONTEXT

This wonderful story of the Samaritan woman who finds Jesus reinforces the Gospel's main theme: that Jesus is the Messiah and Son of God. The thrust of these verses is not so much the woman's conversion but that Jesus is Messiah. Important also is the fact that this chapter demonstrates Jesus' love and understanding of people. His love for humankind knows no boundaries, for He lovingly and compassionately reaches out to a woman who is a social outcast. In contrast to the limitations of human love, Christ exhibits the character of divine love that is indiscriminate and all-encompassing.

By recording Jesus' explanation of this encounter to His disciples, John gives five subtle but genuine proofs that Jesus is truly Messiah and Son of God:

1. proof from His immediate control of everything (v. 27)

2. proof from His impact on the woman (vv. 28–30)

3. proof from His intimacy with the Father (vv. 31–34)

4. proof from His insight into human souls (vv. 35–38)

5. proof from His impression on the Samaritans (vv. 39–42)

The episode of Jesus' healing the official's son at the end of the chapter constitutes the second major "sign" (of eight signs) that John uses to reinforce Jesus' true identity.

KEYS TO THE TEXT

Samaria/Samaritans: When the nation of Israel split politically after Solomon's rule, King Omri named the capital of the northern kingdom of Israel "Samaria" (1 Kin. 16:24). The name eventually referred to the entire district which had been taken captive by Assyria in 722 BC. While Assyria led most of the populace of the ten northern tribes away (into the region which today is northern Iraq), it left a sizable population of Jews in the northern Samaritan region and then transported many non-Jews into Samaria. These groups intermingled to form a mixed race through intermarriage. Eventually tension developed between the Samaritans and the Jews who returned from captivity. The Samaritans withdrew from the worship of Yahweh at Jerusalem and established their worship at Mt. Gerizim in Samaria. Samaritans regarded only the Pentateuch as authoritative. As a result of this history, Jews repudiated the Samaritans and considered them heretical. Intense ethnic and cultural tensions raged historically between the two groups so that both avoided contact as much as possible.

UNLEASHING THE TEXT

Read 4:1–54, noting the key words and definitions next to the passage.

He left Judea (v. 3)—Most likely, Jesus wanted to avoid any possible trouble with John's disciples and the Pharisees who were troubled with His growing popularity.

He needed to go through (v. 4)—Jesus may have wanted to save time and needless steps; more likely, with this Gospel's repeated emphasis on His doing the will of the Father, the idea is probably that Jesus had a divine appointment with the Samaritan woman.

Sychar (v. 5)—This town is probably identified with the modern village of Askar on the shoulder of Mt. Ebal, opposite Mt. Gerizim. A continuous line of tradition identifies Jacob's well as lying about a half mile south of Askar.

wearied from His journey (v. 6)—Jesus, in His humanity, suffered from physical limitations.

John 4:1–54 (NKJV)

1 *Therefore, when the Lord knew that the Pharisees had heard that Jesus made and baptized more disciples than John*

2 *(though Jesus Himself did not baptize, but His disciples),*

3 *He left Judea and departed again to Galilee.*

4 *But He needed to go through Samaria.*

5 *So He came to a city of Samaria which is called Sychar, near the plot of ground that Jacob gave to his son Joseph.*

6 *Now Jacob's well was there. Jesus therefore, being wearied from His journey, sat thus by the well. It was about the sixth hour.*

7 *A woman of Samaria came to draw water. Jesus said to her, "Give Me a drink."*

8 *For His disciples had gone away into the city to buy food.*

9 *Then the woman of Samaria said to Him, "How is it that You, being a Jew, ask a drink from me, a*

Samaritan woman?" For Jews have no dealings with Samaritans.

10 Jesus answered and said to her, "If you knew the gift of God, and who it is who says to you, 'Give Me a drink,' you would have asked Him, and He would have given you living water."

11 The woman said to Him, "Sir, You have nothing to draw with, and the well is deep. Where then do You get that living water?

12 Are You greater than our father Jacob, who gave us the well, and drank from it himself, as well as his sons and his livestock?"

13 Jesus answered and said to her, "Whoever drinks of this water will thirst again,

14 but whoever drinks of the water that I shall give him will never thirst. But the water that I shall give him will become in him a fountain of water springing up into everlasting life."

15 The woman said to Him, "Sir, give me this water, that I may not thirst, nor come here to draw."

16 Jesus said to her, "Go, call your husband, and come here."

17 The woman answered and said, "I have no husband." Jesus said to her, "You have well said, 'I have no husband,'

18 for you have had five husbands, and the one whom you now have is not your husband; in that you spoke truly."

19 The woman said to Him, "Sir, I perceive that You are a prophet.

20 Our fathers worshiped on this mountain, and you Jews say that in Jerusalem is the place where one ought to worship."

21 Jesus said to her, "Woman, believe Me, the hour is coming when you will neither on this mountain, nor in Jerusalem, worship the Father.

22 You worship what you do not know; we know what we worship, for salvation is of the Jews.

23 But the hour is coming, and now is, when the true worshipers will worship the Father in spirit and

a woman of Samaria came to draw water (v. 7)—Women generally came in groups either early or late in the day; this solitary female coming at midday highlights her public shame.

Give me a drink (v. 7)—Jesus, a Jewish man and rabbi, violated all sorts of social taboos by speaking publicly to a Samaritan woman of questionable morals.

living water (v. 10)—an allusion to a common Old Testament metaphor that referred to the knowledge of God and His grace that, in turn, provided cleansing, spiritual life, and power through the Spirit of God; Jesus was using this woman's physical thirst as an object lesson regarding deeper spiritual realities.

call your husband (v. 16)—Jesus abruptly turned the dialogue to focus sharply on her real spiritual need for conversion and cleansing from sin.

not your husband (v. 18)—Biblically, marriage is always restricted to a public, formal, official, and recognized covenant.

on this mountain (v. 20)—The Samaritans, who recognized only the Pentateuch (and not the whole Hebrew canon), regarded Mount Gerizim, the site of Abraham's first altar to God, as the only appropriate place for worship.

you do not know (v. 22)—Because the Samaritans did not know God, they did not have the full revelation of Him and thus could not worship in truth.

true worshipers (v. 23)—In light of the coming of Messiah and Savior, worshipers are identified not by a particular shrine or location but by their worship from the heart of the Father through the Son.

God is Spirit (v. 24)—God is invisible and immaterial and thereby unknowable by material man until He chooses to reveal Himself.

in spirit and truth (v. 24)—God-honoring worship doesn't merely conform to external religious rituals but must flow from hearts that are right with God and lives that are consistent with Scripture.

I who speak to you am He (v. 26)—a forthright claim to be Messiah

to the men (v. 28)—Suddenly the woman who avoided public contact was seeking out her fellow townspeople to tell them about Christ.

My food is to do the will of Him who sent Me (v. 34)—When Jesus talked with the woman, he was performing the will of the Father and thereby received deep spiritual sustenance and satisfaction.

truth; for the Father is seeking such to worship Him.

24 *God is Spirit, and those who worship Him must worship in spirit and truth."*

25 *The woman said to Him, "I know that Messiah is coming" (who is called Christ). "When He comes, He will tell us all things."*

26 *Jesus said to her, "I who speak to you am He."*

27 *And at this point His disciples came, and they marveled that He talked with a woman; yet no one said, "What do You seek?" or, "Why are You talking with her?"*

28 *The woman then left her waterpot, went her way into the city, and said to the men,*

29 *"Come, see a Man who told me all things that I ever did. Could this be the Christ?"*

30 *Then they went out of the city and came to Him.*

31 *In the meantime His disciples urged Him, saying, "Rabbi, eat."*

32 *But He said to them, "I have food to eat of which you do not know."*

33 *Therefore the disciples said to one another, "Has anyone brought Him anything to eat?"*

34 *Jesus said to them, "My food is to do the will of Him who sent Me, and to finish His work.*

35 *Do you not say, 'There are still four months and then comes the harvest'? Behold, I say to you, lift up your eyes and look at the fields, for they are already white for harvest!*

36 *And he who reaps receives wages, and gathers fruit for eternal life, that both he who sows and he who reaps may rejoice together.*

37 *For in this the saying is true: 'One sows and another reaps.'*

38 *I sent you to reap that for which you have not labored; others have labored, and you have entered into their labors."*

39 *And many of the Samaritans of that city believed in Him because of the word of the woman who testified, "He told me all that I ever did."*

40 *So when the Samaritans had come to Him, they urged Him to stay with them; and He stayed there two days.*

41 *And many more believed because of His own word.*

42 *Then they said to the woman, "Now we believe, not because of what you said, for we ourselves have heard Him and we know that this is indeed the Christ, the Savior of the world."*

43 *Now after the two days He departed from there and went to Galilee.*

44 *For Jesus Himself testified that a prophet has no honor in his own country.*

45 *So when He came to Galilee, the Galileans received Him, having seen all the things He did in Jerusalem at the feast; for they also had gone to the feast.*

46 *So Jesus came again to Cana of Galilee where He had made the water wine. And there was a certain nobleman whose son was sick at Capernaum.*

47 *When he heard that Jesus had come out of Judea into Galilee, he went to Him and implored Him to come down and heal his son, for he was at the point of death.*

48 *Then Jesus said to him, "Unless you people see signs and wonders, you will by no means believe."*

49 *The nobleman said to Him, "Sir, come down before my child dies!"*

50 *Jesus said to him, "Go your way; your son lives." So the man believed the word that Jesus spoke to him, and he went his way.*

51 *And as he was now going down, his servants met him and told him, saying, "Your son lives!"*

52 *Then he inquired of them the hour when he got better. And they said to him, "Yesterday at the seventh hour the fever left him."*

53 *So the father knew that it was at the same hour in which Jesus said to him, "Your son lives." And he himself believed, and his whole household.*

54 *This again is the second sign Jesus did when He had come out of Judea into Galilee.*

Savior of the world (v. 42)—Christ came not just for the Jews but also for people of other cultures.

Unless you people see signs and wonders (v. 48)—Jesus castigated the Galileans for their disregard of the person of Christ and their obsession with His works.

33

1) How would you describe the woman at the well? What do you observe about her that impresses you?

_____

_____

_____

_____

2) What did Jesus mean by the phrase "living water" (v. 10)?

_____

_____

_____

_____

(Verses to consider: Ezek. 36:25–27; Zech. 14:8–9)

3) How did Jesus describe God, His Father, in the conversation with the Samaritan woman? What are the implications of this truth?

_____

_____

_____

(Verses to consider: Col. 1:15; 1 Tim. 1:17; Heb. 11:27)

GOING DEEPER

Read Jeremiah 2:1–13 and consider how this passage relates to Jesus' reference to "living water."

EXPLORING THE MEANING

4) Why do you think the Jews of the Old Testament and the Jews of John's Gospel missed out on the living water offered by Christ?

_____

_____

_____

_____

5) Put in your own words what Jesus meant when He spoke of never thirsting again.

_____

_____

_____

6) What is the significance of Jesus' claim that "I have food to eat of which you do not know"?

_____

_____

_____

7) How is doing God's will filling and satisfying?

_____

_____

_____

(Verses to consider: Deut. 8:3; Matt. 4:4)

Truth for Today

When a person is saved, sanctified, submissive, suffering, and thankful, he is already in God's will. "Delight yourself also in the Lord and He shall give you the desires of your heart" (Ps. 37:4 NKJV), David tells us. In other words, when we are what God wants us to be, He is in control, and our will is merged with His will, and He therefore gives us the desires He has planted in our hearts. Jesus is our supreme example. He always functioned according to the divine principles established by the Father.

Reflecting on the Text

8) Why did John add the account of the healing of the nobleman's son? What purpose does this incident serve in John's overall argument for who Jesus is?

_____

_____

_____

9) What lessons in evangelism—sharing the good news with others—can we learn from Christ's encounter with the Samaritan woman at Jacob's well? From the Samaritan woman's encounter with her own townspeople?

_____

_____

_____

10) How do you know what God's will is? How can Jesus' example help you discover God's will?

_____

_____

_____

PERSONAL RESPONSE

Write out additional reflections, questions you may have, or a prayer.

_____

_____

_____

_____

_____

_____

_____

_____

_____

_____

_____

_____

_____

_____

5

UNHEEDED MIRACLES

DRAWING NEAR

What does it mean to hunger and thirst spiritually?

How do you tend to fill your spiritual longings?

THE CONTEXT

This section of John's Gospel begins the shift from reservation and hesitation about Jesus as Messiah to outright rejection. The opposition begins with the controversy regarding Jesus' healing of the paralytic man on the Sabbath. Following this miracle, Jesus confronts the Jews' religious hypocrisy with clear statements about His deity. For the first time, John reveals the murderous intent of the Jewish leaders.

In chapter six, John records Christ's feeding of the five thousand. This is the fourth "sign" in John's Gospel, and the only miracle recorded in all four Gospels. Not only does this miracle display and demonstrate Christ's power and deity, but it also sets the stage for Jesus' controversial discourse about being the "bread of life." The broad opposition to Christ intensifies in chapter 6, as many of His disciples turn away.

KEYS TO THE TEXT

Blasphemy: The act of cursing, slandering, reviling, or showing contempt or lack of reverence for God. In the Old Testament, blaspheming God was a serious crime punishable by death (Lev. 24:15–16). The unbelieving Jews of Jesus' day charged Him with blasphemy because they thought of Him only as a man, but He claimed to be equal with God. Jesus' acceptance of messiahship and deity had always brought vigorous opposition from the Jewish leaders. Later, the charge of blasphemy was central in Jesus' trial before Caiaphas. (*Nelson's New Illustrated Bible Dictionary*)

Signs: These are miracles that point to the power of God behind them—marvels have no value unless they point to God and His truth. The Gospel of John identifies eight miracles that constitute "signs"—confirmation or proofs that reinforce Jesus' true identity: (1) turning water into wine (2:1–11); (2) healing the royal official's son (4:46–54); (3) healing the lame man (5:1–18); (4) feeding the multitude (6:1–15); (5) walking on water (6:16–21); (6) healing the blind man (9:1–41); (7) raising Lazarus from the dead (11:1–57); and (8) the miraculous catch of fish after Jesus' resurrection (21:6–11). Each of the eight miracles was different; no two were alike. The purpose was to convince his readers of Jesus' true identity as the incarnate God-man.

Unleashing the Text

Read 5:1–6:71, noting the key words and definitions next to the passage.

feast of the Jews (v. 1)—John does not specify which particular Jewish feast.

lay (v. 3)—It was customary for the sick to recline at this particular pool, which was thought to have miraculous curative powers.

5:3b, 4—The latter half of v. 3 along with v. 4 are not original to the Gospel. The earliest and best Greek manuscripts, as well as the early versions, exclude the reading. The presence of words or expressions unfamiliar to John's writings also militate against its inclusion.

thirty-eight years (v. 5)—a particularly grave, long-term condition

knew (v. 6)—implies supernatural, intimate awareness of the man's situation

John 5:1–6:71 (NKJV)

1 After this there was a feast of the Jews, and Jesus went up to Jerusalem.

2 Now there is in Jerusalem by the Sheep Gate a pool, which is called in Hebrew, Bethesda, having five porches.

3 In these lay a great multitude of sick people, blind, lame, paralyzed, waiting for the moving of the water.

4 For an angel went down at a certain time into the pool and stirred up the water; then whoever stepped in first, after the stirring of the water, was made well of whatever disease he had.

5 Now a certain man was there who had an infirmity thirty-eight years.

6 When Jesus saw him lying there, and knew that he already had been in that condition a long time, He said to him, "Do you want to be made well?"

7 The sick man answered Him, "Sir, I have no man to put me into the pool when the water is stirred up; but while I am coming, another steps down before me."

8 Jesus said to him, "Rise, take up your bed and walk."

9 And immediately the man was made well, took up his bed, and walked.

10 *The Jews therefore said to him who was cured, "It is the Sabbath; it is not lawful for you to carry your bed."*

11 *He answered them, "He who made me well said to me, 'Take up your bed and walk.' "*

12 *Then they asked him, "Who is the Man who said to you, 'Take up your bed and walk'?"*

13 *But the one who was healed did not know who it was, for Jesus had withdrawn, a multitude being in that place.*

14 *Afterward Jesus found him in the temple, and said to him, "See, you have been made well. Sin no more, lest a worse thing come upon you."*

15 *The man departed and told the Jews that it was Jesus who had made him well.*

16 *For this reason the Jews persecuted Jesus, and sought to kill Him, because He had done these things on the Sabbath.*

17 *But Jesus answered them, "My Father has been working until now, and I have been working."*

18 *Therefore the Jews sought all the more to kill Him, because He not only broke the Sabbath, but also said that God was His Father, making Himself equal with God.*

19 *Then Jesus answered and said to them, "Most assuredly, I say to you, the Son can do nothing of Himself, but what He sees the Father do; for whatever He does, the Son also does in like manner.*

20 *For the Father loves the Son, and shows Him all things that He Himself does; and He will show Him greater works than these, that you may marvel.*

21 *For as the Father raises the dead and gives life to them, even so the Son gives life to whom He will.*

22 *For the Father judges no one, but has committed all judgment to the Son,*

23 *that all should honor the Son just as they honor the Father. He who does not honor the Son does not honor the Father who sent Him.*

24 *"Most assuredly, I say to you, he who hears My word and believes in Him who sent Me has everlasting*

It is not lawful (v. 10)—Normal work was forbidden on the Sabbath by Old Testament law; the rabbinical oral tradition which had developed over time legalistically, piously, and hypocritically expanded this prohibition to include almost every activity; thus the man broke oral tradition, not the Old Testament law.

persecuted (v. 16)—The verb suggests repeated, continued hostile activity.

Most assuredly (v. 19)—an emphatic way of saying, "I'm telling you the truth"

honor the Son just as they honor the Father (v. 23)—Jesus was not a mere ambassador acting in the name of a monarch; He possessed full and complete equality with the Father.

hour is coming, and now is (v. 25)—the already/not yet tension of those who are spiritually resurrected in Christ and yet await a future, physical resurrection

those who have done good . . . evil (v. 29)—not a statement of justification by works; in the context, the "good" is believing on the Son so as to receive a new nature

the very works I do (v. 36)—Christ's works were witness to His deity and messiahship

life, and shall not come into judgment, but has passed from death into life.

25 *Most assuredly, I say to you, the hour is coming, and now is, when the dead will hear the voice of the Son of God; and those who hear will live.*

26 *For as the Father has life in Himself, so He has granted the Son to have life in Himself,*

27 *and has given Him authority to execute judgment also, because He is the Son of Man.*

28 *Do not marvel at this; for the hour is coming in which all who are in the graves will hear His voice*

29 *and come forth— those who have done good, to the resurrection of life, and those who have done evil, to the resurrection of condemnation.*

30 *I can of Myself do nothing. As I hear, I judge; and My judgment is righteous, because I do not seek My own will but the will of the Father who sent Me.*

31 *"If I bear witness of Myself, My witness is not true.*

32 *There is another who bears witness of Me, and I know that the witness which He witnesses of Me is true.*

33 *You have sent to John, and he has borne witness to the truth.*

34 *Yet I do not receive testimony from man, but I say these things that you may be saved.*

35 *He was the burning and shining lamp, and you were willing for a time to rejoice in his light.*

36 *But I have a greater witness than John's; for the works which the Father has given Me to finish—the very works that I do—bear witness of Me, that the Father has sent Me.*

37 *And the Father Himself, who sent Me, has testified of Me. You have neither heard His voice at any time, nor seen His form.*

38 *But you do not have His word abiding in you, because whom He sent, Him you do not believe.*

39 *You search the Scriptures, for in them you think you have eternal life; and these are they which testify of Me.*

40 *But you are not willing to come to Me that you may have life.*

41 *"I do not receive honor from men.*

42 *But I know you, that you do not have the love of God in you.*

43 *I have come in My Father's name, and you do not receive Me; if another comes in his own name, him you will receive.*

44 *How can you believe, who receive honor from one another, and do not seek the honor that comes from the only God?*

45 *Do not think that I shall accuse you to the Father; there is one who accuses you—Moses, in whom you trust.*

46 *For if you believed Moses, you would believe Me; for he wrote about Me.*

47 *But if you do not believe his writings, how will you believe My words?"*

6:1 *After these things Jesus went over the Sea of Galilee, which is the Sea of Tiberias.*

2 *Then a great multitude followed Him, because they saw His signs which He performed on those who were diseased.*

3 *And Jesus went up on the mountain, and there He sat with His disciples.*

4 *Now the Passover, a feast of the Jews, was near.*

5 *Then Jesus lifted up His eyes, and seeing a great multitude coming toward Him, He said to Philip, "Where shall we buy bread, that these may eat?"*

6 *But this He said to test him, for He Himself knew what He would do.*

7 *Philip answered Him, "Two hundred denarii worth of bread is not sufficient for them, that every one of them may have a little."*

8 *One of His disciples, Andrew, Simon Peter's brother, said to Him,*

9 *"There is a lad here who has five barley loaves and two small fish, but what are they among so many?"*

10 *Then Jesus said, "Make the people sit down." Now there was much grass in the place. So the men sat down, in number about five thousand.*

I do not receive honor from men (v. 41)—Christ refused to be the kind of Messiah the Jews sought, choosing instead to do only what pleased God.

him you will receive (v. 43)—The Jewish historian Josephus cited a string of messianic pretenders in the years before AD 70 who were able to gain followings.

After these things (6:1)—A large gap of time may exist between chapters 5 and 6.

two hundred denarii (v. 7)—eight months' wages

five thousand (v. 10)—the number of men only; the actual total may have approached 20,000

41

the Prophet (v. 14)—a reference to Deuteronomy 18, indicating the people's desire for a Messiah who would meet physical, not spiritual, needs

a great wind was blowing (v. 18)—Cooler air rushing down from the mountains onto the warm, moist surface of the Sea of Galilee (some seven hundred feet below sea level) commonly produces a violent churning effect.

immediately the boat was at the land (v. 21)—The boat miraculously and instantaneously arrived at its destination.

11 And Jesus took the loaves, and when He had given thanks He distributed them to the disciples, and the disciples to those sitting down; and likewise of the fish, as much as they wanted.

12 So when they were filled, He said to His disciples, "Gather up the fragments that remain, so that nothing is lost."

13 Therefore they gathered them up, and filled twelve baskets with the fragments of the five barley loaves which were left over by those who had eaten.

14 Then those men, when they had seen the sign that Jesus did, said, "This is truly the Prophet who is to come into the world."

15 Therefore when Jesus perceived that they were about to come and take Him by force to make Him king, He departed again to the mountain by Himself alone.

16 Now when evening came, His disciples went down to the sea,

17 got into the boat, and went over the sea toward Capernaum. And it was already dark, and Jesus had not come to them.

18 Then the sea arose because a great wind was blowing.

19 So when they had rowed about three or four miles, they saw Jesus walking on the sea and drawing near the boat; and they were afraid.

20 But He said to them, "It is I; do not be afraid."

21 Then they willingly received Him into the boat, and immediately the boat was at the land where they were going.

22 On the following day, when the people who were standing on the other side of the sea saw that there was no other boat there, except that one which His disciples had entered, and that Jesus had not entered the boat with His disciples, but His disciples had gone away alone—

23 however, other boats came from Tiberias, near the place where they ate bread after the Lord had given thanks—

24 when the people therefore saw that Jesus was not

there, nor His disciples, they also got into boats and came to Capernaum, seeking Jesus.

25 And when they found Him on the other side of the sea, they said to Him, "Rabbi, when did You come here?"

26 Jesus answered them and said, "Most assuredly, I say to you, you seek Me, not because you saw the signs, but because you ate of the loaves and were filled.

27 Do not labor for the food which perishes, but for the food which endures to everlasting life, which the Son of Man will give you, because God the Father has set His seal on Him."

food which perishes (v. 27)—a rebuke due to the crowd's preference for physical, and not spiritual, blessings

28 Then they said to Him, "What shall we do, that we may work the works of God?"

29 Jesus answered and said to them, "This is the work of God, that you believe in Him whom He sent."

the work of God that you believe (v. 29)—The only work God desired was faith or trust in Jesus as Messiah and Son of God.

30 Therefore they said to Him, "What sign will You perform then, that we may see it and believe You? What work will You do?

31 Our fathers ate the manna in the desert; as it is written, 'He gave them bread from heaven to eat.'"

32 Then Jesus said to them, "Most assuredly, I say to you, Moses did not give you the bread from heaven, but My Father gives you the true bread from heaven.

true bread from heaven (v. 32)—The Old Testament manna was a meager shadow of Christ, the real, eternal, spiritual food of God.

33 For the bread of God is He who comes down from heaven and gives life to the world."

34 Then they said to Him, "Lord, give us this bread always."

35 And Jesus said to them, "I am the bread of life. He who comes to Me shall never hunger, and he who believes in Me shall never thirst.

36 But I said to you that you have seen Me and yet do not believe.

37 All that the Father gives Me will come to Me, and the one who comes to Me I will by no means cast out.

All that the Father gives me will come to Me (v. 37)—a clear statement of God's sovereignty in the selection of those who will be saved

38 For I have come down from heaven, not to do My own will, but the will of Him who sent Me.

39 This is the will of the Father who sent Me, that of all He has given Me I should lose nothing, but should raise it up at the last day.

everyone who sees the Son and believes in Him (v. 40)—an emphasis on the human responsibility in salvation; God works through exercised faith (though even that faith is a gift)

draws him (v. 44)—Scripture clearly indicates that no "free will" exists in man's fallen, depraved nature; humans are unable to believe apart from God's empowerment.

quarreled (v. 52)—The veiled sayings of Jesus sparked conflict among the Jews who did not see beyond a mere physical perspective.

eat . . . drink (v. 53)—Eating Christ's flesh and drinking His blood are metaphorical symbols of the need to accept His work on the cross.

40 And this is the will of Him who sent Me, that everyone who sees the Son and believes in Him may have everlasting life; and I will raise him up at the last day."

41 The Jews then complained about Him, because He said, "I am the bread which came down from heaven."

42 And they said, "Is not this Jesus, the son of Joseph, whose father and mother we know? How is it then that He says, 'I have come down from heaven'?"

43 Jesus therefore answered and said to them, "Do not murmur among yourselves.

44 No one can come to Me unless the Father who sent Me draws him; and I will raise him up at the last day.

45 It is written in the prophets, 'And they shall all be taught by God.' Therefore everyone who has heard and learned from the Father comes to Me.

46 Not that anyone has seen the Father, except He who is from God; He has seen the Father.

47 Most assuredly, I say to you, he who believes in Me has everlasting life.

48 I am the bread of life.

49 Your fathers ate the manna in the wilderness, and are dead.

50 This is the bread which comes down from heaven, that one may eat of it and not die.

51 I am the living bread which came down from heaven. If anyone eats of this bread, he will live forever; and the bread that I shall give is My flesh, which I shall give for the life of the world."

52 The Jews therefore quarreled among themselves, saying, "How can this Man give us His flesh to eat?"

53 Then Jesus said to them, "Most assuredly, I say to you, unless you eat the flesh of the Son of Man and drink His blood, you have no life in you.

54 Whoever eats My flesh and drinks My blood has eternal life, and I will raise him up at the last day.

55 For My flesh is food indeed, and My blood is drink indeed.

56 *He who eats My flesh and drinks My blood abides in Me, and I in him.*

57 *As the living Father sent Me, and I live because of the Father, so he who feeds on Me will live because of Me.*

58 *This is the bread which came down from heaven— not as your fathers ate the manna, and are dead. He who eats this bread will live forever."*

59 *These things He said in the synagogue as He taught in Capernaum.*

60 *Therefore many of His disciples, when they heard this, said, "This is a hard saying; who can understand it?"*

61 *When Jesus knew in Himself that His disciples complained about this, He said to them, "Does this offend you?*

62 *What then if you should see the Son of Man ascend where He was before?*

63 *It is the Spirit who gives life; the flesh profits nothing. The words that I speak to you are spirit, and they are life.*

64 *But there are some of you who do not believe." For Jesus knew from the beginning who they were who did not believe, and who would betray Him.*

65 *And He said, "Therefore I have said to you that no one can come to Me unless it has been granted to him by My Father."*

66 *From that time many of His disciples went back and walked with Him no more.*

67 *Then Jesus said to the twelve, "Do you also want to go away?"*

68 *But Simon Peter answered Him, "Lord, to whom shall we go? You have the words of eternal life.*

69 *Also we have come to believe and know that You are the Christ, the Son of the living God."*

70 *Jesus answered them, "Did I not choose you, the twelve, and one of you is a devil?"*

71 *He spoke of Judas Iscariot, the son of Simon, for it was he who would betray Him, being one of the twelve.*

disciples walked with Him no more (v. 66)—a final, decisive abandonment

devil (v. 70)—literally, a "slanderer" or "false accuser"; this reference to Judas implies the way in which the supreme adversary of God is able to operate behind and through the decisions of fallen human beings

1) How exactly did Jesus cure the paralytic man? What was significant about this?

_____

_____

_____

_____

2) How did the Jews react to this remarkable miracle? Why?

_____

_____

_____

3) What four witnesses did Jesus cite as testifying to His identity as the Messiah/Son of God? (See 5:31–47)

_____

_____

_____

(Verses to consider: John 10:25; Luke 3:22)

4) Skim the passage, and describe all the places Jesus traveled throughout this passage. Look them up on a Bible map if possible.

_____

_____

_____

GOING DEEPER

Read Matthew 23:1–33 and consider Jesus' assessment of the Jewish religious leaders who began to openly oppose Him in chapters 5 and 6.

Exploring the Meaning

5) What dangers of organized religion does this passage in Matthew highlight?

_____

_____

_____

_____

6) What was the reaction of the masses to Christ's feeding of the five thousand? In what ways is this still a common response to Jesus?

_____

_____

_____

_____

(Verses to consider: Matt. 10:34–39; John 18:36; Acts 3:22, 23)

7) Summarize in your own words what Christ meant when He said, "I am the bread of life." In what ways have you experienced this truth?

_____

_____

_____

_____

Truth for Today

Salvation is not through a creed, a church, a ritual, a pastor, a priest, or any other such human means—but through Jesus Christ, who said, Come to Me. To come is to believe to the point of submitting to His lordship. "I am the bread of life," Jesus declared; "He who comes to Me shall not hunger, and he who believes in Me shall never thirst" (6:35). The words *come* and *believe* are parallel, just as are *hunger* and *thirst*. Coming to Christ is believing in Him, which results in no longer hungering and thirsting. Other biblical synonyms for believing in Christ include confessing Him, receiving Him, eating and drinking Him, and hearing Him.

Reflecting on the Text

8) Recount the time when you first came to Jesus and believed. How has He satisfied your soul?

_____

_____

_____

9) According to John 6:37–44, 65, who is responsible for our salvation? What are the implications of this?

_____

_____

_____

(Verses to consider: Rom. 3:1–19; Eph. 2:1–9)

10) When in your life have you seen the greatest example of the power of God? How has that strengthened your faith?

_____

_____

_____

Personal Response

Write out additional reflections, questions you may have, or a prayer.

_____

_____

_____

_____

_____

_____

_____

_____

6

REACTIONS TO THE SON OF GOD

DRAWING NEAR

Jesus used many metaphors to help explain who He was and why He came.
"I am the door. I am the Good Shepherd. I am the way. I am the light."
Which of these images is most encouraging to you right now? Why?

I'm the light. In this way, t
time is a dark time and it
is reassuring to know that
I have the returning light.

THE CONTEXT

The main thrust of this section of John's Gospel can be summarized as high-intensity hatred, as the smoldering dislike of Christ erupts into a blazing inferno. Chapters 7 and 8 focus on Jesus at the Feast of Tabernacles in Jerusalem. The two major themes associated with this feast (water and light) come to prominence in this section. The central truth that dominates this entire passage is that Jesus was on a divine timetable. He lived according to God's sovereign and perfect timing and direction.

Chapter 9 features the healing of the man with congenital blindness. Not only does this "sign" point again to the fact that Jesus is Messiah/Son of God, but it also underlines the blindness of the hyper-religious Jews due to their callous unbelief. The characteristics of unbelief are seen clearly here:

1) unbelief sets false standards;
2) unbelief always wants more evidence but never has enough;
3) unbelief does biased research on a purely subjective basis;
4) unbelief rejects obvious facts;
5) and unbelief is self-centered.

Jesus' discourse on being the Good Shepherd in chapter 10 flows directly from chapter 9. Christ addressed the same group of people, those false shepherds who were leading the nation astray from the true knowledge and kingdom of Messiah. In contrast to these self-appointed and self-righteous impostors, God had appointed the sinless Christ as Savior and King. As you read through this lengthy passage, you will be drawn up in the heightening drama. Ask God to show you more and more who Jesus is.

KEYS TO THE TEXT

Stoning: The usual method of capital punishment in ancient Israel. People who broke specific statutes of the law of Moses were put to death by stoning. Stoning was usually carried out by the men of the community, upon the testimony of at least two witnesses, who would then cast the first stones (Deut. 17:5–7; John 8:7; Acts 7:58). Stoning usually took place outside the settlement or camp. Acts punishable by stoning were certain cases of disobedience, child sacrifice, consultation with magicians, blasphemy, breaking the Sabbath, the worship of false gods, rebellion against parents, and adultery. (*Nelson's New Illustrated Bible Dictionary*)

Jewish Religious Leaders: Referred to in John as "the Jews" in various places, this group was variously made up of Pharisees, Sadducees, scribes, and teachers of the law. The Pharisees were a small legalistic sect of the Jews, who were known for their rigid adherence to the ceremonial fine points of the law. The *Sadducees* denied the resurrection of the dead and the existence of angels, and accepted only the Pentateuch as authoritative. In the days of Herod, their sect controlled the temple. Jesus rebuked them for using human tradition to nullify Scripture and for rank hypocrisy.

UNLEASHING THE TEXT

Read 7:1–10:42, noting the key words and definitions next to the passage.

John 7:1–10:42 (NKJV)

After these things (v. 1)—A seven month gap likely took place between chapters 6 and 7.

Feast of Tabernacles (v. 2)—Associated in the Old Testament with the ingathering of the grape harvest, this festival was known for water-drawing and lamp-lighting rites.

My time has not yet come (v. 6)—Jesus lived with absolute dependence and commitment to the Father's perfect time-table.

1 After these things Jesus walked in Galilee; for He did not want to walk in Judea, because the Jews sought to kill Him.

2 Now the Jews' Feast of Tabernacles was at hand.

3 His brothers therefore said to Him, "Depart from here and go into Judea, that Your disciples also may see the works that You are doing.

4 For no one does anything in secret while he himself seeks to be known openly. If You do these things, show Yourself to the world."

5 For even His brothers did not believe in Him.

6 Then Jesus said to them, "My time has not yet come, but your time is always ready.

7 The world cannot hate you, but it hates Me because I testify of it that its works are evil.

8 *You go up to this feast. I am not yet going up to this feast, for My time has not yet fully come."*

9 *When He had said these things to them, He remained in Galilee.*

10 *But when His brothers had gone up, then He also went up to the feast, not openly, but as it were in secret.*

11 *Then the Jews sought Him at the feast, and said, "Where is He?"*

12 *And there was much complaining among the people concerning Him. Some said, "He is good"; others said, "No, on the contrary, He deceives the people."*

13 *However, no one spoke openly of Him for fear of the Jews.*

14 *Now about the middle of the feast Jesus went up into the temple and taught.*

15 *And the Jews marveled, saying, "How does this Man know letters, having never studied?"*

16 *Jesus answered them and said, "My doctrine is not Mine, but His who sent Me.*

17 *If anyone wills to do His will, he shall know concerning the doctrine, whether it is from God or whether I speak on My own authority.*

18 *He who speaks from himself seeks his own glory; but He who seeks the glory of the One who sent Him is true, and no unrighteousness is in Him.*

19 *Did not Moses give you the law, yet none of you keeps the law? Why do you seek to kill Me?"*

20 *The people answered and said, "You have a demon. Who is seeking to kill You?"*

21 *Jesus answered and said to them, "I did one work, and you all marvel.*

22 *Moses therefore gave you circumcision (not that it is from Moses, but from the fathers), and you circumcise a man on the Sabbath.*

23 *If a man receives circumcision on the Sabbath, so that the law of Moses should not be broken, are you angry with Me because I made a man completely well on the Sabbath?*

middle of the feast (v. 14)—Jesus may have waited in order to avoid an attempt by the crowd to pressure Him into some kind of premature presentation as Messiah.

marveled (v. 15)—Jesus' knowledge of the Scripture (despite not having been formally trained) astounded the Jews.

If anyone wills to do His will, he shall know (v. 17)—Those who are fundamentally committed to doing God's will shall be guided by Him in the affirmation of His truth.

He speaks boldly (v. 26)—The masses were surprised by Jesus' bold proclamations in the face of opposition by the nation's religious leaders.

no one knows where He is from (v. 27)—A tradition had developed in Jewish circles (based on a misinterpretation of Isaiah 53:8 and Malachi 3:1) that the identity of Messiah would be wholly unknown until He appeared and redeemed the nation. Jesus' background in Nazareth was documented.

where I am you cannot come (v. 34)—a reference to His return to heaven after the crucifixion and resurrection

If anyone thirsts (v. 37)—The Feast of Tabernacles featured priests carrying containers filled with water, accompanied by music and Scripture reading to symbolize the blessing of rainfall. Jesus was using an object lesson to invite the people to quench their spiritual thirst, reminiscent of Isaiah 55:1.

24 *Do not judge according to appearance, but judge with righteous judgment."*

25 *Now some of them from Jerusalem said, "Is this not He whom they seek to kill?*

26 *But look! He speaks boldly, and they say nothing to Him. Do the rulers know indeed that this is truly the Christ?*

27 *However, we know where this Man is from; but when the Christ comes, no one knows where He is from."*

28 *Then Jesus cried out, as He taught in the temple, saying, "You both know Me, and you know where I am from; and I have not come of Myself, but He who sent Me is true, whom you do not know.*

29 *But I know Him, for I am from Him, and He sent Me."*

30 *Therefore they sought to take Him; but no one laid a hand on Him, because His hour had not yet come.*

31 *And many of the people believed in Him, and said, "When the Christ comes, will He do more signs than these which this Man has done?"*

32 *The Pharisees heard the crowd murmuring these things concerning Him, and the Pharisees and the chief priests sent officers to take Him.*

33 *Then Jesus said to them, "I shall be with you a little while longer, and then I go to Him who sent Me.*

34 *You will seek Me and not find Me, and where I am you cannot come."*

35 *Then the Jews said among themselves, "Where does He intend to go that we shall not find Him? Does He intend to go to the Dispersion among the Greeks and teach the Greeks?*

36 *What is this thing that He said, 'You will seek Me and not find Me, and where I am you cannot come'?"*

37 *On the last day, that great day of the feast, Jesus stood and cried out, saying, "If anyone thirsts, let him come to Me and drink.*

38 *He who believes in Me, as the Scripture has said, out of his heart will flow rivers of living water."*

39 *But this He spoke concerning the Spirit, whom those believing in Him would receive; for the Holy Spirit was not yet given, because Jesus was not yet glorified.*

40 *Therefore many from the crowd, when they heard this saying, said, "Truly this is the Prophet."*

41 *Others said, "This is the Christ." But some said, "Will the Christ come out of Galilee?*

42 *Has not the Scripture said that the Christ comes from the seed of David and from the town of Bethlehem, where David was?"*

43 *So there was a division among the people because of Him.*

44 *Now some of them wanted to take Him, but no one laid hands on Him.*

45 *Then the officers came to the chief priests and Pharisees, who said to them, "Why have you not brought Him?"*

46 *The officers answered, "No man ever spoke like this Man!"*

47 *Then the Pharisees answered them, "Are you also deceived?*

48 *Have any of the rulers or the Pharisees believed in Him?*

49 *But this crowd that does not know the law is accursed."*

50 *Nicodemus (he who came to Jesus by night, being one of them) said to them,*

51 *"Does our law judge a man before it hears him and knows what he is doing?"*

52 *They answered and said to him, "Are you also from Galilee? Search and look, for no prophet has arisen out of Galilee."*

53 *And everyone went to his own house.*

8:1 *But Jesus went to the Mount of Olives.*

2 *Now early in the morning He came again into the temple, and all the people came to Him; and He sat down and taught them.*

3 *Then the scribes and Pharisees brought to Him a woman caught in adultery. And when they had set her in the midst,*

out of Galilee (v. 41)—Jesus was born in Bethlehem, not Galilee—the crowd was too lazy to examine Christ's true credentials.

Now early in the morning (8:2)—The episode with the adulteress is not found in the earliest, most reliable manuscripts; nevertheless, many believe it is authentic.

He who is without sin (v. 7)—a reference to Deuteronomy 13:9 and 17:7 where the witnesses of a crime were required to start the execution

sin no more (v. 11)—actually, "leave your life of sin"

I am the light of the world (v.12)—The Old Testament indicates that in the coming age of Messiah the Lord will be a light for His people.

4 they said to Him, "Teacher, this woman was caught in adultery, in the very act.

5 Now Moses, in the law, commanded us that such should be stoned. But what do You say?"

6 This they said, testing Him, that they might have something of which to accuse Him. But Jesus stooped down and wrote on the ground with His finger, as though He did not hear.

7 So when they continued asking Him, He raised Himself up and said to them, "He who is without sin among you, let him throw a stone at her first."

8 And again He stooped down and wrote on the ground.

9 Then those who heard it, being convicted by their conscience, went out one by one, beginning with the oldest even to the last. And Jesus was left alone, and the woman standing in the midst.

10 When Jesus had raised Himself up and saw no one but the woman, He said to her, "Woman, where are those accusers of yours? Has no one condemned you?"

11 She said, "No one, Lord." And Jesus said to her, "Neither do I condemn you; go and sin no more."

12 Then Jesus spoke to them again, saying, "I am the light of the world. He who follows Me shall not walk in darkness, but have the light of life."

13 The Pharisees therefore said to Him, "You bear witness of Yourself; Your witness is not true."

14 Jesus answered and said to them, "Even if I bear witness of Myself, My witness is true, for I know where I came from and where I am going; but you do not know where I come from and where I am going.

15 You judge according to the flesh; I judge no one.

16 And yet if I do judge, My judgment is true; for I am not alone, but I am with the Father who sent Me.

17 It is also written in your law that the testimony of two men is true.

18 I am One who bears witness of Myself, and the Father who sent Me bears witness of Me."

19 Then they said to Him, "Where is Your Father?" Jesus answered, "You know neither Me nor My Father. If you had known Me, you would have known My Father also."

20 These words Jesus spoke in the treasury, as He taught in the temple; and no one laid hands on Him, for His hour had not yet come.

21 Then Jesus said to them again, "I am going away, and you will seek Me, and will die in your sin. Where I go you cannot come."

22 So the Jews said, "Will He kill Himself, because He says, 'Where I go you cannot come'?"

23 And He said to them, "You are from beneath; I am from above. You are of this world; I am not of this world.

24 Therefore I said to you that you will die in your sins; for if you do not believe that I am He, you will die in your sins."

25 Then they said to Him, "Who are You?" And Jesus said to them, "Just what I have been saying to you from the beginning.

26 I have many things to say and to judge concerning you, but He who sent Me is true; and I speak to the world those things which I heard from Him."

27 They did not understand that He spoke to them of the Father.

28 Then Jesus said to them, "When you lift up the Son of Man, then you will know that I am He, and that I do nothing of Myself; but as My Father taught Me, I speak these things.

29 And He who sent Me is with Me. The Father has not left Me alone, for I always do those things that please Him."

30 As He spoke these words, many believed in Him.

31 Then Jesus said to those Jews who believed Him, "If you abide in My word, you are My disciples indeed.

32 And you shall know the truth, and the truth shall make you free."

33 They answered Him, "We are Abraham's

Where is your father? (v. 19)—The Jews were thinking only in naturalistic, physical terms.

You are from beneath (v. 23)—a statement of His opponents' true kinship with Satan and his realm; they were spiritually blinded, thinking they were doing God's will, when just the opposite was true

I am He (v. 24)—He is not part of the original statement; thus this statement is likely a claim to be the I AM of Exodus 3:14.

When you lift up the Son of Man (v. 28)—a reference to the impending crucifixion

the truth (v. 32)—the facts surrounding Jesus and the teaching that He brought

descendants, and have never been in bondage to anyone. How can You say, 'You will be made free'?"

34 Jesus answered them, "Most assuredly, I say to you, whoever commits sin is a slave of sin.

35 And a slave does not abide in the house forever, but a son abides forever.

36 Therefore if the Son makes you free, you shall be free indeed.

37 "I know that you are Abraham's descendants, but you seek to kill Me, because My word has no place in you.

38 I speak what I have seen with My Father, and you do what you have seen with your father."

39 They answered and said to Him, "Abraham is our father." Jesus said to them, "If you were Abraham's children, you would do the works of Abraham.

40 But now you seek to kill Me, a Man who has told you the truth which I heard from God. Abraham did not do this.

41 You do the deeds of your father." Then they said to Him, "We were not born of fornication; we have one Father—God."

42 Jesus said to them, "If God were your Father, you would love Me, for I proceeded forth and came from God; nor have I come of Myself, but He sent Me.

43 Why do you not understand My speech? Because you are not able to listen to My word.

44 You are of your father the devil, and the desires of your father you want to do. He was a murderer from the beginning, and does not stand in the truth, because there is no truth in him. When he speaks a lie, he speaks from his own resources, for he is a liar and the father of it.

45 But because I tell the truth, you do not believe Me.

46 Which of you convicts Me of sin? And if I tell the truth, why do you not believe Me?

47 He who is of God hears God's words; therefore you do not hear, because you are not of God."

If you were Abraham's children (v. 39)—implying that they were not his children in a spiritual sense; that is, they did not imitate his faith and thus were not saved

works of Abraham (v. 39)— Abraham's obedience proved his faith.

your father the devil (v. 44)— The Jewish hostility to the Son of God proved their true paternity.

48 Then the Jews answered and said to Him, "Do we not say rightly that You are a Samaritan and have a demon?"

49 Jesus answered, "I do not have a demon; but I honor My Father, and you dishonor Me.

50 And I do not seek My own glory; there is One who seeks and judges.

51 Most assuredly, I say to you, if anyone keeps My word he shall never see death."

52 Then the Jews said to Him, "Now we know that You have a demon! Abraham is dead, and the prophets; and You say, 'If anyone keeps My word he shall never taste death.'

53 Are You greater than our father Abraham, who is dead? And the prophets are dead. Who do You make Yourself out to be?"

54 Jesus answered, "If I honor Myself, My honor is nothing. It is My Father who honors Me, of whom you say that He is your God.

55 Yet you have not known Him, but I know Him. And if I say, 'I do not know Him,' I shall be a liar like you; but I do know Him and keep His word.

56 Your father Abraham rejoiced to see My day, and he saw it and was glad."

57 Then the Jews said to Him, "You are not yet fifty years old, and have You seen Abraham?"

58 Jesus said to them, "Most assuredly, I say to you, before Abraham was, I AM."

59 Then they took up stones to throw at Him; but Jesus hid Himself and went out of the temple, going through the midst of them, and so passed by.

9:1 Now as Jesus passed by, He saw a man who was blind from birth.

2 And His disciples asked Him, saying, "Rabbi, who sinned, this man or his parents, that he was born blind?"

3 Jesus answered, "Neither this man nor his parents sinned, but that the works of God should be revealed in him.

You are a Samaritan (v. 48)—Unable to refute Jesus' claims, the Jews resorted to name calling.

hid Himself . . . going through the midst of them (v. 59)—probably by supernatural means since the appointed hour of His suffering had not yet come.

who sinned (9:2)—The Jews commonly regarded suffering as proof of sin in the victim's life. Sin can result in suffering, but this is not always the case.

the night is coming (v. 4)—a reference to the seeming triumph of evil during Christ's arrest and crucifixion

made clay with the saliva (v. 6)—an allusion to creation, in which humans were made from the dust of the ground

4 I must work the works of Him who sent Me while it is day; the night is coming when no one can work.

5 As long as I am in the world, I am the light of the world."

6 When He had said these things, He spat on the ground and made clay with the saliva; and He anointed the eyes of the blind man with the clay.

7 And He said to him, "Go, wash in the pool of Siloam" (which is translated, Sent). So he went and washed, and came back seeing.

8 Therefore the neighbors and those who previously had seen that he was blind said, "Is not this he who sat and begged?"

9 Some said, "This is he." Others said, "He is like him." He said, "I am he."

10 Therefore they said to him, "How were your eyes opened?"

11 He answered and said, "A Man called Jesus made clay and anointed my eyes and said to me, 'Go to the pool of Siloam and wash.' So I went and washed, and I received sight."

12 Then they said to him, "Where is He?" He said, "I do not know."

13 They brought him who formerly was blind to the Pharisees.

14 Now it was a Sabbath when Jesus made the clay and opened his eyes.

15 Then the Pharisees also asked him again how he had received his sight. He said to them, "He put clay on my eyes, and I washed, and I see."

16 Therefore some of the Pharisees said, "This Man is not from God, because He does not keep the Sabbath." Others said, "How can a man who is a sinner do such signs?" And there was a division among them.

He is a prophet (v. 17)—The blind man saw that Jesus was much more than a mere man; the sighted, obstinate Pharisees were blinded to that truth.

17 They said to the blind man again, "What do you say about Him because He opened your eyes?" He said, "He is a prophet."

18 But the Jews did not believe concerning him, that

he had been blind and received his sight, until they called the parents of him who had received his sight.

19 And they asked them, saying, "Is this your son, who you say was born blind? How then does he now see?"

20 His parents answered them and said, "We know that this is our son, and that he was born blind;

21 but by what means he now sees we do not know, or who opened his eyes we do not know. He is of age; ask him. He will speak for himself."

22 His parents said these things because they feared the Jews, for the Jews had agreed already that if anyone confessed that He was Christ, he would be put out of the synagogue.

23 Therefore his parents said, "He is of age; ask him."

24 So they again called the man who was blind, and said to him, "Give God the glory! We know that this Man is a sinner."

25 He answered and said, "Whether He is a sinner or not I do not know. One thing I know: that though I was blind, now I see."

26 Then they said to him again, "What did He do to you? How did He open your eyes?"

27 He answered them, "I told you already, and you did not listen. Why do you want to hear it again? Do you also want to become His disciples?"

28 Then they reviled him and said, "You are His disciple, but we are Moses' disciples.

29 We know that God spoke to Moses; as for this fellow, we do not know where He is from."

30 The man answered and said to them, "Why, this is a marvelous thing, that you do not know where He is from; yet He has opened my eyes!

31 Now we know that God does not hear sinners; but if anyone is a worshiper of God and does His will, He hears him.

32 Since the world began it has been unheard of that anyone opened the eyes of one who was born blind.

33 If this Man were not from God, He could do nothing."

Start

Give God the glory! (v. 24)—This means that the authorities wanted the man to own up and admit the truth that Jesus was a sinner because He violated their traditions and threatened their influence.

The man answered . . . opened my eyes! (v. 30)—The healed man demonstrated more spiritual insight and common sense than all of the religious authorities combined who sat in judgment of Jesus and him.

Do you believe (v. 35)—an invitation for the man to put his trust in Jesus as Messiah

For judgment (v. 39)—Though Christ's ultimate purpose was to save, saving some requires condemning others.

sheepfold (10:1)—A sustained metaphor that would have struck a chord in pastoral Palestine, the picture was meant to contrast Jesus the "Good Shepherd" with the false shepherds who presumed to lead Israel religiously.

the sheep hear his voice (v. 3)—Every Near Eastern shepherd had a unique call that his sheep recognized.

I am the door (v. 7)—Christ changed the metaphor to make Himself the gate or entrance— that is, the way to safety and rest.

34 They answered and said to him, "You were completely born in sins, and are you teaching us?" And they cast him out.

35 Jesus heard that they had cast him out; and when He had found him, He said to him, "Do you believe in the Son of God?"

36 He answered and said, "Who is He, Lord, that I may believe in Him?"

37 And Jesus said to him, "You have both seen Him and it is He who is talking with you."

38 Then he said, "Lord, I believe!" And he worshiped Him.

39 And Jesus said, "For judgment I have come into this world, that those who do not see may see, and that those who see may be made blind."

40 Then some of the Pharisees who were with Him heard these words, and said to Him, "Are we blind also?"

41 Jesus said to them, "If you were blind, you would have no sin; but now you say, 'We see.' Therefore your sin remains.

10:1 "Most assuredly, I say to you, he who does not enter the sheepfold by the door, but climbs up some other way, the same is a thief and a robber.

2 But he who enters by the door is the shepherd of the sheep.

3 To him the doorkeeper opens, and the sheep hear his voice; and he calls his own sheep by name and leads them out.

4 And when he brings out his own sheep, he goes before them; and the sheep follow him, for they know his voice.

5 Yet they will by no means follow a stranger, but will flee from him, for they do not know the voice of strangers."

6 Jesus used this illustration, but they did not understand the things which He spoke to them.

7 Then Jesus said to them again, "Most assuredly, I say to you, I am the door of the sheep.

8   All who ever came before Me are thieves and
    robbers, but the sheep did not hear them.

9   I am the door. If anyone enters by Me, he will be
    saved, and will go in and out and find pasture.

10 The thief does not come except to steal, and to kill,
    and to destroy. I have come that they may have life,
    and that they may have it more abundantly.

11 "I am the good shepherd. The good shepherd gives
    His life for the sheep.

12 But a hireling, he who is not the shepherd, one who
    does not own the sheep, sees the wolf coming and
    leaves the sheep and flees; and the wolf catches the
    sheep and scatters them.

13 The hireling flees because he is a hireling and does
    not care about the sheep.

14 I am the good shepherd; and I know My sheep, and
    am known by My own.

15 As the Father knows Me, even so I know the Father;
    and I lay down My life for the sheep.

16 And other sheep I have which are not of this fold;
    them also I must bring, and they will hear My voice;
    and there will be one flock and one shepherd.

17 "Therefore My Father loves Me, because I lay down
    My life that I may take it again.

18 No one takes it from Me, but I lay it down of Myself.
    I have power to lay it down, and I have power to
    take it again. This command I have received from
    My Father."

19 Therefore there was a division again among the Jews
    because of these sayings.

20 And many of them said, "He has a demon and is
    mad. Why do you listen to Him?"

21 Others said, "These are not the words of one who
    has a demon. Can a demon open the eyes of the
    blind?"

22 Now it was the Feast of Dedication in Jerusalem,
    and it was winter.

23 And Jesus walked in the temple, in Solomon's porch.

24 Then the Jews surrounded Him and said to Him,

sees the wolf coming . . . flees (v. 12)—The hireling (that is, the religious leaders in the metaphor) does not display sacrificial care for the sheep in times of danger.

Feast of Dedication (v. 22)—the Jewish celebration of Hanukkah, also called the Feast of Lights, a commemoration of Israel's victory over Antiochus Epiphanes during the Maccabean Revolt (166–142 BC)

tell us plainly (v. 24)—not a request for clarity but an attempt to get Jesus to make a public statement for which they could accuse Him of blasphemy

"How long do You keep us in doubt? If You are the Christ, tell us plainly."

25 Jesus answered them, "I told you, and you do not believe. The works that I do in My Father's name, they bear witness of Me.

26 But you do not believe, because you are not of My sheep, as I said to you.

27 My sheep hear My voice, and I know them, and they follow Me.

28 And I give them eternal life, and they shall never perish; neither shall anyone snatch them out of My hand.

29 My Father, who has given them to Me, is greater than all; and no one is able to snatch them out of My Father's hand.

I and my Father are one (v. 30)—a statement of unity in nature and essence

30 I and My Father are one."

31 Then the Jews took up stones again to stone Him.

32 Jesus answered them, "Many good works I have shown you from My Father. For which of those works do you stone Me?"

33 The Jews answered Him, saying, "For a good work we do not stone You, but for blasphemy, and because You, being a Man, make Yourself God."

34 Jesus answered them, "Is it not written in your law, 'I said, "You are gods"'?

Scripture cannot be broken (v. 35)—an affirmation of the absolute accuracy and authority of Scripture

35 If He called them gods, to whom the word of God came (and the Scripture cannot be broken),

36 do you say of Him whom the Father sanctified and sent into the world, 'You are blaspheming,' because I said, 'I am the Son of God'?

37 If I do not do the works of My Father, do not believe Me;

38 but if I do, though you do not believe Me, believe the works, that you may know and believe that the Father is in Me, and I in Him."

39 Therefore they sought again to seize Him, but He escaped out of their hand.

40 And He went away again beyond the Jordan to the place where John was baptizing at first, and there He stayed.

41 *Then many came to Him and said, "John performed no sign, but all the things that John spoke about this Man were true."*

42 *And many believed in Him there.*

1) What did Jesus' family (specifically his brothers) think of Him? What clues do you find here to support your answer?

Mark 3,21 — for he is out hi mind did not believe on him either

(Verse to consider: Mark 3:21)

2) What was the crowd's response to Christ's teaching (7:14–19)? How did Jesus characterize His own teaching?

did n

3) What did the Pharisees claim about Christ (8:13–59)—that is, His identity and nature? What did Jesus in turn say about *their* true nature?

4) What is significant about what Jesus shouted out on the last day of the Feast of Tabernacles? (See 7:37–39)

(Verses to consider: Isa. 12:3; 55:1; Zech. 13:1)

GOING DEEPER

The metaphor of water is used throughout the Bible to express God's power to heal and save. Read Ezekiel 47:1–9, keeping in mind Jesus' statement in 7:37–39.

EXPLORING THE MEANING

5) How do Jesus' claims to offer "living water" and to be the "light of the world" tie into Old Testament prophecies and allusions? Explain what He meant.

(Verses to consider: Exod. 13:21, 22; 14:19–20; Ps. 27:1; 119:105; Prov. 6:23; Isa. 42:6–7; 49:6; Ezek. 1:26–28; Mal. 4:2)

6) What truth is revealed by the fact that the Jews and Pharisees would not believe in Christ even when faced with the man who had been miraculously healed of his blindness by Jesus?

how hard hearted they were

7) What type of freedom was Jesus talking about in 8:36?

spiritual free

TRUTH FOR TODAY

When we preach, teach, and witness that Christ is the only way to God, we are not proclaiming our own view of right religion but God's revelation of truth. We do not proclaim the narrow way simply because we are already in it, or because it happens to suit our temperament, or because we are bigoted and exclusive. We proclaim the narrow way because it is God's way and God's only way for people to find salvation and eternal life. We proclaim a narrow gospel because Jesus said, "I am the door; if anyone enters through Me, he shall be saved" (10:9).

Reflecting on the Text

8) Jesus claimed to be the Good Shepherd. What does that mean? How can this truth make a practical and tangible difference in your life this week?

9) What does the story of the adulterous woman (8:1–11) reveal about Christ? About forgiveness and grace? About pride? About repentance?

10) As the self-proclaimed "light of the world," Jesus speaks blunt truth to the darkened hearts of sinful people. Will we hear and obey? Or, like the Pharisees, will we resist and reject the hard truth of God? In what area(s) of your life do you sense the Lord speaking uncomfortable words to you? What will you do?

Personal Response

Write out additional reflections, questions you may have, or a prayer.

ADDITIONAL NOTES

7

THE RESURRECTION AND THE LIFE

DRAWING NEAR

What, if any, fears or distresses about death do you have?

No fears for me – just want to know my family will be cared

What have you learned about Jesus thus far that helps to allay these fears?

Jesus will Care for all, He will be here for my fr

THE CONTEXT

At the beginning of chapter 11, we find Jesus standing in the shadow of the cross. His little time in the area beyond the Jordan had ended. John picked up the story after Jesus moved back into the area of Jerusalem, with His death on the cross only a few days away.

In those last few days before His death, the scene changes from hatred and rejection (10:39) to an unmistakable and blessed witness of the glory of Christ. All the rejection and hatred of the Jews could not dim Christ's glory as displayed through the resurrection of Lazarus. This miracle is the climactic and most dramatic sign in the Gospel of John and is the capstone of Jesus' public ministry. As such, it evidences His glory in at least three ways:

1) It pointed clearly to His deity.
2) It strengthened the faith of His disciples.
3) It led directly to the cross (12:23).

As you read about this amazing miracle and the reactions to it, ask God to help you understand more deeply the truths spoken by Jesus.

Keys to the Text

Mary and Martha: This is the first mention of this family in John. Clearly they were good friends of Jesus and He stayed with them several times. John related the story of Mary's anointing of Jesus later, in 12:1–8, but that may indicate that the original readers were already familiar with the event. In Luke 10:38–42, Jesus came to their house for dinner. Martha was busy doing many things supposedly for Jesus' sake, but Mary was sitting humbly at Jesus' feet.

Caiaphas: The high priest was the supreme religious head of his people, distinguished from his fellow priests by the clothes he wore, the duties he performed, and the particular requirements placed upon him. Caiaphas served as high priest from AD 18 to 36, an unusually long tenure for anyone in that role. His longevity suggests he had a close relationship with both Rome and the Herodian dynasty. He was son-in-law to his predecessor, Annas. He controlled the temple and no doubt personally profited from the corrupt merchandising that was taking place there. His enmity against Jesus seems intensely personal and especially malevolent; every time he appears in Scripture, he is seeking Jesus' destruction.

Unleashing the Text

Read 11:1–54, noting the key words and definitions next to the passage.

Bethany (v. 1)—Different from the Bethany mentioned in 1:28, this village is on the east side of the Mount of Olives, two miles from Jerusalem, along the road to Jericho.

he whom You love (v. 3)—a touching hint of the close friendship between Jesus and Lazarus

the Son of God may be glorified (v. 4)—The real purpose behind Lazarus' illness was not death, but glory.

He stayed two more days (v. 6)—The delay was due to the fact that Jesus loved this family; this love would be clear as He would greatly strengthen their faith by raising Lazarus. The delay would also dispel rumors that the resurrection was a hoax.

John 11:1–54 (NKJV)

1 Now a certain man was sick, Lazarus of Bethany, the town of Mary and her sister Martha.

2 It was that Mary who anointed the Lord with fragrant oil and wiped His feet with her hair, whose brother Lazarus was sick.

3 Therefore the sisters sent to Him, saying, "Lord, behold, he whom You love is sick."

4 When Jesus heard that, He said, "This sickness is not unto death, but for the glory of God, that the Son of God may be glorified through it."

5 Now Jesus loved Martha and her sister and Lazarus.

6 So, when He heard that he was sick, He stayed two more days in the place where He was.

7 Then after this He said to the disciples, "Let us go to Judea again."

8 The disciples said to Him, "Rabbi, lately the Jews

sought to stone You, and are You going there
again?"

9 Jesus answered, "Are there not twelve hours in
the day? If anyone walks in the day, he does not
stumble, because he sees the light of this world.

10 But if one walks in the night, he stumbles, because
the light is not in him."

11 These things He said, and after that He said to them,
"Our friend Lazarus sleeps, but I go that I may
wake him up."

sleeps (v. 11)—a euphemistic term used in the New Testament to refer to death, especially in regard to believers who will be resurrected

12 Then His disciples said, "Lord, if he sleeps he will get
well."

13 However, Jesus spoke of his death, but they thought
that He was speaking about taking rest in sleep.

14 Then Jesus said to them plainly, "Lazarus is dead.

15 And I am glad for your sakes that I was not there,
that you may believe. Nevertheless let us go to him."

16 Then Thomas, who is called the Twin, said to his
fellow disciples, "Let us also go, that we may die
with Him."

17 So when Jesus came, He found that he had already
been in the tomb four days.

in the tomb (v. 17)—a stone sepulcher, probably a hewn-out cave

four days (v. 17)—This emphasizes the magnitude of the miracle because the Jews did not embalm and the body would already be in a rapid state of decay.

18 Now Bethany was near Jerusalem, about two miles
away.

19 And many of the Jews had joined the women
around Martha and Mary, to comfort them
concerning their brother.

20 Now Martha, as soon as she heard that Jesus was
coming, went and met Him, but Mary was sitting in
the house.

21 Now Martha said to Jesus, "Lord, if You had been
here, my brother would not have died.

22 But even now I know that whatever You ask of God,
God will give You."

23 Jesus said to her, "Your brother will rise again."

24 Martha said to Him, "I know that he will rise again
in the resurrection at the last day."

25 Jesus said to her, "I am the resurrection and the life.
He who believes in Me, though he may die, he shall
live.

I am the resurrection and the life (v. 25)—the fifth in the series of seven "I am" statements in John; the idea is that no resurrection or eternal life exists outside of the Son of God; He is the source of both

the Jews who came with her weeping (v. 33)—a combination of friends, relatives, and professional mourners; funeral customs required families to hire at least two flute players and a professional wailing woman to mourn the dead

He groaned in His spirit and was troubled (v. 33)—The Greek term "groaned" always suggests anger, outrage, or emotional indignation. Most likely Jesus was angered at the grief of the people in that it revealed their deep unbelief; they were grieving as pagans with no hope.

Jesus wept (v. 35)—a silent bursting into tears as opposed to a loud lament or wailing; Christ wept for the fallen world, entangled in sin and all its consequences

stench (v. 39)—The Jews did not embalm, but rather used aromatic spices to countereffect the repulsive odor of bodily decay.

26 And whoever lives and believes in Me shall never die. Do you believe this?"

27 She said to Him, "Yes, Lord, I believe that You are the Christ, the Son of God, who is to come into the world."

28 And when she had said these things, she went her way and secretly called Mary her sister, saying, "The Teacher has come and is calling for you."

29 As soon as she heard that, she arose quickly and came to Him.

30 Now Jesus had not yet come into the town, but was in the place where Martha met Him.

31 Then the Jews who were with her in the house, and comforting her, when they saw that Mary rose up quickly and went out, followed her, saying, "She is going to the tomb to weep there."

32 Then, when Mary came where Jesus was, and saw Him, she fell down at His feet, saying to Him, "Lord, if You had been here, my brother would not have died."

33 Therefore, when Jesus saw her weeping, and the Jews who came with her weeping, He groaned in the spirit and was troubled.

34 And He said, "Where have you laid him?" They said to Him, "Lord, come and see."

35 Jesus wept.

36 Then the Jews said, "See how He loved him!"

37 And some of them said, "Could not this Man, who opened the eyes of the blind, also have kept this man from dying?"

38 Then Jesus, again groaning in Himself, came to the tomb. It was a cave, and a stone lay against it.

39 Jesus said, "Take away the stone." Martha, the sister of him who was dead, said to Him, "Lord, by this time there is a stench, for he has been dead four days."

40 Jesus said to her, "Did I not say to you that if you would believe you would see the glory of God?"

41 Then they took away the stone from the place where

the dead man was lying. And Jesus lifted up His eyes and said, "Father, I thank You that You have heard Me.

42 And I know that You always hear Me, but because of the people who are standing by I said this, that they may believe that You sent Me."

43 Now when He had said these things, He cried with a loud voice, "Lazarus, come forth!"

44 And he who had died came out bound hand and foot with graveclothes, and his face was wrapped with a cloth. Jesus said to them, "Loose him, and let him go."

45 Then many of the Jews who had come to Mary, and had seen the things Jesus did, believed in Him.

46 But some of them went away to the Pharisees and told them the things Jesus did.

47 Then the chief priests and the Pharisees gathered a council and said, "What shall we do? For this Man works many signs.

48 If we let Him alone like this, everyone will believe in Him, and the Romans will come and take away both our place and nation."

49 And one of them, Caiaphas, being high priest that year, said to them, "You know nothing at all,

50 nor do you consider that it is expedient for us that one man should die for the people, and not that the whole nation should perish."

51 Now this he did not say on his own authority; but being high priest that year he prophesied that Jesus would die for the nation,

52 and not for that nation only, but also that He would gather together in one the children of God who were scattered abroad.

53 Then, from that day on, they plotted to put Him to death.

54 Therefore Jesus no longer walked openly among the Jews, but went from there into the country near the wilderness, to a city called Ephraim, and there remained with His disciples.

the Romans will come (v. 48)—The Jews feared that escalating Messianic expectations could start a movement against Roman oppression and occupation that would cause the Romans to move harshly against the Jewish people.

one man should die for the people (v. 50)—Caiaphas unwittingly used sacrificial, substitutionary language, prophesying the death of Christ for sinners.

gather together in one the children of God (v. 52)—a reference to believing Jews who had been dispersed from the Promised Land, as well as Gentiles who would form the church

from that day on (v. 53)—The Jewish leaders' minds were made up and their course of action fixed: They would seek to eliminate Christ.

1) What evidence in chapter 11 leads you to believe that Jesus had an especially close relationship with Lazarus and his sisters?

_____

_____

_____

2) Why do you think the text describes Jesus as "groaning" in His spirit, weeping, and being troubled over the death of Lazarus—especially if Jesus knew that He was going to bring Lazarus back to life?

_____

_____

_____

_____

3) What do you learn about Jesus' humanity from this passage? About His divinity?

_____

_____

_____

4) As the Pharisees plotted to kill Jesus, Caiphas made what unwitting, profound remark (v. 50)? How was this prophetic?

_____

_____

_____

GOING DEEPER

Go back and read John 3:16–21, reviewing the statements and promises that Jesus made. Compare it to what you have discovered here in John 11.

Exploring the Meaning

5) What added insights into the doctrine of the resurrection do you gain from the passage in John 3?

_____

_____

_____

_____

6) In what ways did Jesus' raising of Lazarus foreshadow future events?

_____

_____

_____

7) Skim over Revelation 21:1–48. What does this passage teach about death and the future state?

_____

_____

_____

_____

Truth for Today

Since the Fall, there has been a curse on the earth and that curse has sent the earth and all of its inhabitants careening and spiraling into disasters, tears, sickness, and the grave. Sin was not God's purpose for man. All things in the world were created for the good and blessing of man, but sin corrupted that goodness and blessing and brought a curse instead. In God's time sin will one day have run its course and be forever destroyed. "Behold, the tabernacle of God is with men, and He shall dwell with them, and they shall be His people. God Himself will be with them and He will wipe away every tear from their eyes; and there shall be no more death; nor sorrow, nor crying. There shall be no more pain, for the former things have passed away" (Rev. 21:3–4 NKJV).

Reflecting on the Text

8) Clearly Lazarus and his sisters enjoyed an intimate friendship with Jesus. What do you think is the secret to that kind of relationship with Christ?

_____

_____

_____

9) How does Christ's statement that He is the "resurrection and the life" change the way you view death?

_____

_____

_____

10) What friends or family members do you know who are grieving the death of a loved one? How specifically can you pray for them and encourage them in the coming days?

_____

_____

_____

Personal Response

Write out additional reflections, questions you may have, or a prayer.

_____

_____

_____

_____

_____

_____

_____

_____

8

THE KING ENTERS JERUSALEM

DRAWING NEAR

In what way has this study of John helped you see Jesus with fresh eyes? What new things about Him have you learned?

_____

_____

_____

THE CONTEXT

This section of John's Gospel contrasts the differing reactions of love and hate, belief and rejection of Christ, leading up to the tumultuous events of Jesus' arrest, trial, and crucifixion.

Following the record of Mary's anointing of Christ, John notes the events surrounding Christ's triumphal entry into Jerusalem on Palm Sunday. This is one of only a few incidents that are mentioned in all four Gospels. It is significant because by this action Jesus presented Himself officially to the nation as the Messiah and Son of God.

The Sanhedrin and other Jewish leaders wanted Jesus dead but did not want Him killed during the Passover time because they feared stirring up the multitudes with whom He was popular. Jesus entered the city, however, on His own time and forced the whole issue in order that it might happen exactly on the Passover day when the lambs were being sacrificed. As the Scripture says, "Christ, our Passover, was sacrificed for us" (1 Cor. 5:7; 1 Pet. 1:19). In God's perfect timing, at the precise time foreordained from eternity, Jesus Christ presented Himself to die.

KEYS TO THE TEXT

Passover Feast: The Passover was a very special feast day in Israel's religious calendar and was inextricably linked to what took place in the Exodus (Exod. 12–13). It became entrenched in Israel's tradition and has always marked the day of redemption from Egypt. Passover began with the slaying of the Passover lamb, which had to be a lamb without blemish. Friday of Passover would have begun on Thursday at sunset. According to Josephus, it was customary in his day to slay the lamb at about 3 PM. This was the time of day that Christ, the Christian's Passover lamb, died (1 Cor. 5:7; Luke 23:44–46).

UNLEASHING THE TEXT

Read 11:55–12:50, noting the key words and definitions next to the passage.

John 11:55–12:50 (NKJV)

55 *And the Passover of the Jews was near, and many went from the country up to Jerusalem before the Passover, to purify themselves.*

56 *Then they sought Jesus, and spoke among themselves as they stood in the temple, "What do you think— that He will not come to the feast?"*

if anyone knew (v. 57)—The plotters ensured that the whole city was filled with potential informants.

57 *Now both the chief priests and the Pharisees had given a command, that if anyone knew where He was, he should report it, that they might seize Him.*

12:1 *Then, six days before the Passover, Jesus came to Bethany, where Lazarus was who had been dead, whom He had raised from the dead.*

2 *There they made Him a supper; and Martha served, but Lazarus was one of those who sat at the table with Him.*

a pound of very costly oil of spikenard (12:3)—actually about twelve ounces of an oil extracted from the root of an exotic plant grown in India

anointed the feet of Jesus (v. 3)—This was possible because diners would recline when eating, their feet pointed away from the table. This act symbolized Mary's extravagant love for and devotion to Christ.

3 *Then Mary took a pound of very costly oil of spikenard, anointed the feet of Jesus, and wiped His feet with her hair. And the house was filled with the fragrance of the oil.*

4 *But one of His disciples, Judas Iscariot, Simon's son, who would betray Him, said,*

5 *"Why was this fragrant oil not sold for three hundred denarii and given to the poor?"*

three hundred denarii (v. 5)—a year's wages for a common laborer

a thief (v. 6)—As the band's treasurer, Judas secretly pilfered money for his own use.

6 *This he said, not that he cared for the poor, but because he was a thief, and had the money box; and he used to take what was put in it.*

7 *But Jesus said, "Let her alone; she has kept this for the day of My burial.*

kept this for the day of My burial (v. 7)—As with the earlier statement by Caiaphas, the listeners did not realize the deeper implications of Mary's action.

8 *For the poor you have with you always, but Me you do not have always."*

9 *Now a great many of the Jews knew that He was there; and they came, not for Jesus' sake only, but*

that they might also see Lazarus, whom He had raised from the dead.

10 *But the chief priests plotted to put Lazarus to death also,*

11 *because on account of him many of the Jews went away and believed in Jesus.*

12 *The next day a great multitude that had come to the feast, when they heard that Jesus was coming to Jerusalem,*

13 *took branches of palm trees and went out to meet Him, and cried out: "Hosanna! 'Blessed is He who comes in the name of the Lord!' The King of Israel!"*

14 *Then Jesus, when He had found a young donkey, sat on it; as it is written:*

15 *"Fear not, daughter of Zion; Behold, your King is coming, Sitting on a donkey's colt."*

16 *His disciples did not understand these things at first; but when Jesus was glorified, then they remembered that these things were written about Him and that they had done these things to Him.*

17 *Therefore the people, who were with Him when He called Lazarus out of his tomb and raised him from the dead, bore witness.*

18 *For this reason the people also met Him, because they heard that He had done this sign.*

19 *The Pharisees therefore said among themselves, "You see that you are accomplishing nothing. Look, the world has gone after Him!"*

20 *Now there were certain Greeks among those who came up to worship at the feast.*

21 *Then they came to Philip, who was from Bethsaida of Galilee, and asked him, saying, "Sir, we wish to see Jesus."*

22 *Philip came and told Andrew, and in turn Andrew and Philip told Jesus.*

23 *But Jesus answered them, saying, "The hour has come that the Son of Man should be glorified.*

24 *Most assuredly, I say to you, unless a grain of wheat falls into the ground and dies, it remains alone; but if it dies, it produces much grain.*

took branches of palm trees (v. 13)—Waving palm branches (plentiful in supply in and near Jerusalem) had become a nationalistic symbol and a signal that a messianic liberator had arrived.

Hosanna (v. 13)—a transliteration of the Hebrew word that means "give salvation now!"; a term of acclamation and praise

the world has gone after Him (v. 19)—people in general, not everyone in particular

certain Greeks (v. 20)—Gentile proselytes who had come to Jerusalem for Passover and who, in their desire to see Christ, stood in antithesis to the national leaders, who sought to kill Jesus.

hour (v. 23)—a reference to the time of Jesus' death, resurrection, and exaltation

My soul is troubled (v. 27)—The term used suggests strong horror, anxiety, and agitation; the thought of taking on the wrath of God for the sins of the world created revulsion in the sinless Savior.

glorify Your name (v. 28)—a succinct statement of the principle by which Jesus lived and died

the ruler of this world (v. 31)—a reference to Satan

lifted up from the earth (v. 32)—a reference to the crucifixion

remains forever (v. 34)—Perhaps the people had in mind Old Testament prophecies about the eternal nature of Messiah's kingdom.

that the word of the prophet might be fulfilled (v. 38)—The people's unbelief was both foreseen and necessitated by Scripture; although God predestined such judgment, it was not apart from human responsibility and culpability.

25 *He who loves his life will lose it, and he who hates his life in this world will keep it for eternal life.*

26 *If anyone serves Me, let him follow Me; and where I am, there My servant will be also. If anyone serves Me, him My Father will honor.*

27 *"Now My soul is troubled, and what shall I say? 'Father, save Me from this hour'? But for this purpose I came to this hour.*

28 *Father, glorify Your name." Then a voice came from heaven, saying, "I have both glorified it and will glorify it again."*

29 *Therefore the people who stood by and heard it said that it had thundered. Others said, "An angel has spoken to Him."*

30 *Jesus answered and said, "This voice did not come because of Me, but for your sake.*

31 *Now is the judgment of this world; now the ruler of this world will be cast out.*

32 *And I, if I am lifted up from the earth, will draw all peoples to Myself."*

33 *This He said, signifying by what death He would die.*

34 *The people answered Him, "We have heard from the law that the Christ remains forever; and how can You say, 'The Son of Man must be lifted up'? Who is this Son of Man?"*

35 *Then Jesus said to them, "A little while longer the light is with you. Walk while you have the light, lest darkness overtake you; he who walks in darkness does not know where he is going.*

36 *While you have the light, believe in the light, that you may become sons of light." These things Jesus spoke, and departed, and was hidden from them.*

37 *But although He had done so many signs before them, they did not believe in Him,*

38 *that the word of Isaiah the prophet might be fulfilled, which he spoke: "Lord, who has believed our report? And to whom has the arm of the Lord been revealed?"*

39 *Therefore they could not believe, because Isaiah said again:*

40 *"He has blinded their eyes and hardened their hearts, Lest they should see with their eyes, Lest they should understand with their hearts and turn, So that I should heal them."*

41 *These things Isaiah said when he saw His glory and spoke of Him.*

Isaiah . . . saw His glory and spoke of Him (v. 41)—a reference to Isaiah 6, identifying Jesus as God or Yahweh of the Old Testament

42 *Nevertheless even among the rulers many believed in Him, but because of the Pharisees they did not confess Him, lest they should be put out of the synagogue;*

43 *for they loved the praise of men more than the praise of God.*

44 *Then Jesus cried out and said, "He who believes in Me, believes not in Me but in Him who sent Me.*

45 *And he who sees Me sees Him who sent Me.*

46 *I have come as a light into the world, that whoever believes in Me should not abide in darkness.*

47 *And if anyone hears My words and does not believe, I do not judge him; for I did not come to judge the world but to save the world.*

48 *He who rejects Me, and does not receive My words, has that which judges him— the word that I have spoken will judge him in the last day.*

49 *For I have not spoken on My own authority; but the Father who sent Me gave Me a command, what I should say and what I should speak.*

50 *And I know that His command is everlasting life. Therefore, whatever I speak, just as the Father has told Me, so I speak."*

1) As Passover began, what were the Jewish leaders busy doing?

Trying to find a legal way to kill Jesus Then to find him & arrest him John 11:57

2) Compare the scenes of Jesus' private life and public life in this passage. What differences or similarities do you find in how Jesus behaves? How He treats people?

Jesus stayed The Same always - the Same to day, Tomorrow & always

3) At the supper described in the first part of chapter 12, how did Mary's attitudes and behavior contrast with Judas'?

4) Why was it significant for Christ to enter Jerusalem at Passover time?

(Verses to consider: John 1:29; 1 Cor. 5:7; 1 Pet. 1:19)

GOING DEEPER

Read Psalm 118:1–29. This "psalm of ascent" (along with Psalms 113–117) was frequently sung by pilgrims as they went up to Jerusalem for special feasts and by the temple choir during Israel's religious festivals.

EXPLORING THE MEANING

5) Describe the tone and mood felt in this psalm of ascent. How does this compare with the scene when Christ entered Jerusalem?

6) Read Zechariah 9:9. If Christ really was Israel's promised Messiah and King, why would He have come riding into town on a donkey instead of a war horse or stallion?

_____

_____

_____

_____

(Verses to consider: Matt. 21:1–11)

7) In this chapter Jesus called Satan "the ruler of this world" (12:31). If this is the case, why don't believers have to be troubled by Satan's power and authority?

_____

_____

_____

_____

Truth for Today

In an act of unmeasured love, Mary poured the perfume. In that adoring testimony of love and honor, Mary poured out her soul in worship even as she poured out the perfume. Being absolutely controlled by adoration for her Lord, she lost all sense of restraint and economy. Mary did not offer that valuable possession to support a program or a ministry but offered it to Christ Himself. She did not selfishly seek a visible and tangible result from her generosity but without hesitation offered her most expensive earthly possession to the Lord in an act of effusive, adoring worship.

Reflecting on the Text

8) Mary demonstrated her love and devotion in a costly, sacrificial way. How can you demonstrate your love for Christ this week?

_____

_____

_____

_____

9) Clearly many religious leaders cared more about their circumstances and position than about the truth about Jesus (12:42–43). What are some specific ways you've seen that modern-day believers "love the praise of men more than the praise of God"?

_____

_____

_____

10) Review 12:23–33, and put in your own words the profound principles Jesus taught about His death? About life springing forth from death?

_____

_____

_____

11) Jesus said He came as a "light." What has His light illuminated in your life that needs changing?

_____

_____

_____

PERSONAL RESPONSE

Write out additional reflections, questions you may have, or a prayer.

_____

_____

_____

_____

_____

_____

_____

_____

WITH CHRIST IN THE UPPER ROOM

DRAWING NEAR

Imagine having a face-to-face dinner with the Lord Jesus Christ. What kinds of topics would you want to discuss with Him? Explain why.

THE CONTEXT

In these chapters leading up to the crucifixion and resurrection of our Lord, John's record looks at Jesus devoting Himself to His own disciples. While chapters 1–12 center on the rejection of Jesus by the nation, chapters 13–17 (commonly called the "Upper Room Discourse" by scholars) center on the handful of people who did receive Him.

Beginning here in chapter 13, Jesus shifts completely from public ministry before the masses to private ministry before a few faithful followers. These events are a record of the farewell words and works of Christ on the same night of His betrayal and arrest. With the cross only one day away, these final acts and conversations comprise Jesus' legacy to His followers. Chapter 14 centers on the promise that Christ is the One who gives believers comfort, not only by virtue of His future return but also in the present via the powerful ministry of the Holy Spirit.

Following the dismissal of Judas, Jesus begins His valedictory address to the remaining eleven disciples. Little did they know that their world was about to be shattered. They would be bewildered, confused, and ridden with anxiety because of the events that would soon transpire. Anticipating the disciples' devastation, Jesus spoke to comfort them.

KEYS TO THE TEXT

Footwashing: The dusty and dirty conditions of the region necessitated the need for footwashing. Although the disciples most likely would have been happy to wash Jesus' feet, they could not conceive of washing each other's feet. This was because in the society of the time, footwashing was reserved for the lowliest of menial servants. Peers did not wash one another's feet, except very rarely and as a mark of great love. Luke points out that they were so busy arguing about who was the greatest of them (22:24), that neither of them stopped to wash their feet. When Jesus moved to wash their feet, they were shocked. His actions serve also as a symbol of spiritual cleansing and a model of Christian humility.

Holy Spirit: The Holy Spirit is the divine agent who creates, sustains, and preserves spiritual life in those who place their trust in Jesus Christ. The Holy Spirit is not merely an influence or an impersonal power emanating from God. He is a person, the third member of the Trinity, equal in every way to God the Father and God the Son. He loves the saints, He communicates with them, teaches, guides, comforts, and chastises them. He can be grieved, quenched, lied to, tested, resisted, and blasphemed. Since Pentecost, the Holy Spirit has indwelt all believers, illuminating their understanding and application of God's Word. He fills them, seals them, communes with them, fellowships with them, intercedes for them, comforts them, admonishes them, sanctifies them, and enables them to resist sin and to serve God.

UNLEASHING THE TEXT

Read 13:1–14:31, noting the key words and definitions next to the passage.

John 13:1–14:31 (NKJV)

to the end (v. 1)—to perfection, that is, with a perfect love

1 Now before the Feast of the Passover, when Jesus knew that His hour had come that He should depart from this world to the Father, having loved His own who were in the world, He loved them to the end.

supper (v. 2)—Passover, on Thursday night after sunset

the devil . . . the heart of Judas (v. 2)—This does not exonerate Judas; his wicked heart desired exactly what the devil desired.

2 And supper being ended, the devil having already put it into the heart of Judas Iscariot, Simon's son, to betray Him,

3 Jesus, knowing that the Father had given all things into His hands, and that He had come from God and was going to God,

4 rose from supper and laid aside His garments, took a towel and girded Himself.

5 After that, He poured water into a basin and began to wash the disciples' feet, and to wipe them with the towel with which He was girded.

6 Then He came to Simon Peter. And Peter said to Him, "Lord, are You washing my feet?"

7 Jesus answered and said to him, "What I am doing

you do not understand now, but you will know after this."

8 Peter said to Him, "You shall never wash my feet!" Jesus answered him, "If I do not wash you, you have no part with Me."

9 Simon Peter said to Him, "Lord, not my feet only, but also my hands and my head!"

10 Jesus said to him, "He who is bathed needs only to wash his feet, but is completely clean; and you are clean, but not all of you."

11 For He knew who would betray Him; therefore He said, "You are not all clean."

12 So when He had washed their feet, taken His garments, and sat down again, He said to them, "Do you know what I have done to you?

13 You call Me Teacher and Lord, and you say well, for so I am.

14 If I then, your Lord and Teacher, have washed your feet, you also ought to wash one another's feet.

15 For I have given you an example, that you should do as I have done to you.

16 Most assuredly, I say to you, a servant is not greater than his master; nor is he who is sent greater than he who sent him.

17 If you know these things, blessed are you if you do them.

18 "I do not speak concerning all of you. I know whom I have chosen; but that the Scripture may be fulfilled, 'He who eats bread with Me has lifted up his heel against Me.'

19 Now I tell you before it comes, that when it does come to pass, you may believe that I am He.

20 Most assuredly, I say to you, he who receives whomever I send receives Me; and he who receives Me receives Him who sent Me."

21 When Jesus had said these things, He was troubled in spirit, and testified and said, "Most assuredly, I say to you, one of you will betray Me."

22 Then the disciples looked at one another, perplexed about whom He spoke.

needs only to wash his feet (v. 10)—The cleansing that Christ performs at salvation needs never to be repeated; however, those who have been cleansed by God's gracious justification need repeated washings in the experiential sense in order to maintain pure fellowship with God.

not all clean (v. 11)—a reference to Judas

an example (v. 15)—a pattern or model of humility

one of the disciples, whom Jesus loved (v. 23)—the first self-reference by John, the author of this Gospel

23 Now there was leaning on Jesus' bosom one of His disciples, whom Jesus loved.

24 Simon Peter therefore motioned to him to ask who it was of whom He spoke.

25 Then, leaning back on Jesus' breast, he said to Him, "Lord, who is it?"

26 Jesus answered, "It is he to whom I shall give a piece of bread when I have dipped it." And having dipped the bread, He gave it to Judas Iscariot, the son of Simon.

Satan entered him (v. 27)—Judas was personally possessed by Satan himself.

27 Now after the piece of bread, Satan entered him. Then Jesus said to him, "What you do, do quickly."

28 But no one at the table knew for what reason He said this to him.

29 For some thought, because Judas had the money box, that Jesus had said to him, "Buy those things we need for the feast," or that he should give something to the poor.

it was night (v. 30)—a notation filled with theological implications, referring to the seeming triumph of the forces of darkness

30 Having received the piece of bread, he then went out immediately. And it was night.

31 So, when he had gone out, Jesus said, "Now the Son of Man is glorified, and God is glorified in Him.

glorified (v. 31)—Jesus looked past the cross, anticipating the glory that He would have with the Father when all was over.

32 If God is glorified in Him, God will also glorify Him in Himself, and glorify Him immediately.

33 Little children, I shall be with you a little while longer. You will seek Me; and as I said to the Jews, 'Where I am going, you cannot come,' so now I say to you.

A new commandment (v. 34)—new in the sense that it was modeled on Christ's own sacrificial love and produced only through the New Covenant by the transforming power of the Holy Spirit

34 A new commandment I give to you, that you love one another; as I have loved you, that you also love one another.

35 By this all will know that you are My disciples, if you have love for one another."

you cannot follow (v. 36)—Only Jesus, as the sinless sacrifice for the trespasses of the world, could go to the cross as a substitute.

36 Simon Peter said to Him, "Lord, where are You going?" Jesus answered him, "Where I am going you cannot follow Me now, but you shall follow Me afterward."

37 Peter said to Him, "Lord, why can I not follow You now? I will lay down my life for Your sake."

38 *Jesus answered him, "Will you lay down your life for My sake? Most assuredly, I say to you, the rooster shall not crow till you have denied Me three times.*

14:1 *"Let not your heart be troubled; you believe in God, believe also in Me.*

2 *In My Father's house are many mansions; if it were not so, I would have told you. I go to prepare a place for you.*

3 *And if I go and prepare a place for you, I will come again and receive you to Myself; that where I am, there you may be also.*

4 *And where I go you know, and the way you know."*

5 *Thomas said to Him, "Lord, we do not know where You are going, and how can we know the way?"*

6 *Jesus said to him, "I am the way, the truth, and the life. No one comes to the Father except through Me.*

7 *"If you had known Me, you would have known My Father also; and from now on you know Him and have seen Him."*

8 *Philip said to Him, "Lord, show us the Father, and it is sufficient for us."*

9 *Jesus said to him, "Have I been with you so long, and yet you have not known Me, Philip? He who has seen Me has seen the Father; so how can you say, 'Show us the Father'?*

10 *Do you not believe that I am in the Father, and the Father in Me? The words that I speak to you I do not speak on My own authority; but the Father who dwells in Me does the works.*

11 *Believe Me that I am in the Father and the Father in Me, or else believe Me for the sake of the works themselves.*

12 *"Most assuredly, I say to you, he who believes in Me, the works that I do he will do also; and greater works than these he will do, because I go to My Father.*

13 *And whatever you ask in My name, that I will do, that the Father may be glorified in the Son.*

14 *If you ask anything in My name, I will do it.*

15 *"If you love Me, keep My commandments.*

troubled (14:1)—Faith in Christ can stop the heart from being agitated.

mansions (v. 2)—literally, "dwelling places, rooms, or even apartments" (in modern terms); all are in the large "Father's house"

greater works than these he will do (v. 12)—greater, not in power, but in extent or scope, due to the indwelling Spirit; the focus is on spiritual, not physical miracles

in My name (v. 13)—not a mere formula to be tacked on the end of a prayer, but a reference to the fact that the believer's prayers should be in accord with God's holy nature and eternal purposes

If you love Me, keep My commandments (v. 15)—Love for Christ is inseparable from obedience.

another (v. 16)—literally "another of the same kind"; that is, someone just like Jesus Himself

Helper (v. 16)—literally "one called alongside to help"

dwells with you and will be in you (v. 17)—indicative of the distinction between the ministry of the Holy Spirit before and after Pentecost; a permanent indwelling

I will come to you . . . you will see Me (vv. 18–19)—a reference first to Christ's resurrection, after which His followers would see Him; also a reference to the mystery of the Trinity: through the Spirit, Christ would be back with His followers

16 And I will pray the Father, and He will give you another Helper, that He may abide with you forever—

17 the Spirit of truth, whom the world cannot receive, because it neither sees Him nor knows Him; but you know Him, for He dwells with you and will be in you.

18 I will not leave you orphans; I will come to you.

19 "A little while longer and the world will see Me no more, but you will see Me. Because I live, you will live also.

20 At that day you will know that I am in My Father, and you in Me, and I in you.

21 He who has My commandments and keeps them, it is he who loves Me. And he who loves Me will be loved by My Father, and I will love him and manifest Myself to him."

22 Judas (not Iscariot) said to Him, "Lord, how is it that You will manifest Yourself to us, and not to the world?"

23 Jesus answered and said to him, "If anyone loves Me, he will keep My word; and My Father will love him, and We will come to him and make Our home with him.

24 He who does not love Me does not keep My words; and the word which you hear is not Mine but the Father's who sent Me.

25 "These things I have spoken to you while being present with you.

26 But the Helper, the Holy Spirit, whom the Father will send in My name, He will teach you all things, and bring to your remembrance all things that I said to you.

27 Peace I leave with you, My peace I give to you; not as the world gives do I give to you. Let not your heart be troubled, neither let it be afraid.

28 You have heard Me say to you, 'I am going away and coming back to you.' If you loved Me, you would rejoice because I said, 'I am going to the Father,' for My Father is greater than I.

29 *"And now I have told you before it comes, that when it does come to pass, you may believe.*
30 *I will no longer talk much with you, for the ruler of this world is coming, and he has nothing in Me.*
31 *But that the world may know that I love the Father, and as the Father gave Me commandment, so I do. Arise, let us go from here."*

1) What spiritual lessons was Jesus trying to teach His followers by washing their feet? Was He successful? How do you know?

_____

_____

_____

_____

2) What is the mood surrounding this last supper? Identify all the varied emotions that are described (13:1–38).

_____

_____

_____

_____

3) How did Jesus attempt to comfort His confused disciples (chapter 14)? What assurances did He give them?

_____

_____

_____

_____

GOING DEEPER

Jesus offered the promise of heaven to His followers. Read 1 Thessalonians 4:13–18 for more insight on this topic.

Exploring the Meaning

4) How do Paul's words in 1 Thessalonians illuminate or shed light on the promise of Christ in 14:1–3? What more do you learn?

_____

_____

_____

_____

_____

5) Why did Jesus call the Old Testament command to love God and each other "a new commandment"?

_____

_____

_____

_____

(Verses to consider: Matt. 22:34–40; Rom. 13:8–10; Gal. 5:14)

6) What would you say to the person who claimed that Jesus is only "a" way to God (among many other possible paths)? (See 14:6)

_____

_____

_____

_____

_____

Truth for Today

It is especially tempting to compromise our commitment when the cost becomes high. But the fact that believers sometimes succumb to disobedience does not alter the truth that the character of the true disciple is manifest in obedience. Although imperfect obedience is inevitable because of the unredeemed flesh, the basic desire and life-direction of the true Christian is obedience to the Lord.

Reflecting on the Text

7) Based on Christ's answer to Judas (not Iscariot) in 14:23, what new insights do you see regarding the importance of obedience?

_____

_____

_____

_____

(Verses to consider: Matt. 7:13–14; Luke 13:22–30; John 10:7–9; Acts 4:12)

8) How does the hope of heaven encourage you? How does that truth affect how you live now?

_____

_____

_____

9) Are there any specific commands of Christ you have been overlooking or ignoring? How can you show your love for Christ this week by obeying?

_____

_____

_____

_____

Personal Response

Write out additional reflections, questions you may have, or a prayer.

_____

_____

_____

_____

_____

_____

Additional Notes

10

WITH CHRIST IN THE GARDEN

DRAWING NEAR

Who is one of the most faithful Christians you've ever known? What was her or his secret?

_____

_____

_____

As you begin this lesson, ask God to show you how to more faithfully abide in Him.

_____

_____

_____

THE CONTEXT

In the hours before His arrest, trial, and execution, Jesus gathered His disciples in a private room in order to teach them some final lessons, remind them of some great truths, and encourage them to trust and obey through the difficult times just ahead.

He continues His teaching in chapter 15 with an extended metaphor from agricultural life about Christian living. This familiar "vine-branches" discourse underscores the necessity of fruitfulness in a believer's life and the impossibility of such an experience without a rich, deep, vital, ongoing relationship with Christ. Those who lived such a life, Christ warned, would experience (just as He had) the world's fierce hatred. But the disciples were not to panic over this prospect.

In chapter 16 they heard the reassuring words that the Spirit of God would come, not only as their Helper and Comforter, but also as the Convicter of all who are antagonistic to the gospel. "Be of good cheer," Christ concluded, "I have overcome the world."

In the final moments before His arrest, Christ prayed for His followers (chapter 17). This recorded prayer (more so than the one taught to the disciples in Matthew 6 and Luke 11) is the real Lord's Prayer. It reveals the true face-to-face communion the Son had with the Father and reveals a detailed account of the content of the communication between God the Father and God the Son. John 17 forms a transition, marking the end of Jesus' earthly ministry and the beginning of His intercessory ministry for believers. In many ways the prayer is a summary of John's entire Gospel.

Keys to the Text

Vine and Branches: Jesus is the vine, and His Father is the vinedresser, or gardener. The disciples are the branches. He was speaking of the eleven disciples who were still with Him as He prepared to go to the Garden of Gethsemane. They were the branches who were remaining with Him to the end. The branches who didn't bear fruit and were cut off are represented by Judas, who had already left in order to betray Jesus to the Jewish leaders later that evening. Jesus used the vine illustration for at least three good reasons. First, His disciples would recognize the analogy immediately because Israel was often referred to as a vine in the Old Testament Scriptures. Second, grapevines grew everywhere in Palestine. When He spoke of pruning procedures, He was describing exactly what vinedressers did to produce good crops of grapes. Third, the vine and branches perfectly illustrate the kind of relationship that must exist between Jesus and anyone who wants to be His disciple. This analogy is for all Christians. For anyone to know life and bear fruit, that person must be connected to Jesus Christ.

Unleashing the Text

Read 15:1–17:26, noting the key words and definitions next to the passage.

John 15:1–17:26 (NKJV)

I am the true vine (v. 1)—the last of the seven claims to deity; that is, the seven "I AM" statements

He takes away (v. 2)—the picture is of a vinedresser getting rid of dead wood; it refers to apostate Christians who never truly believe and who are taken away in judgment

Abide in Me (v. 4)—literally, "remain, stay, or dwell within"; the fruit or evidence of salvation is continuance in service to Christ and His teaching

1 "I am the true vine, and My Father is the vinedresser.

2 Every branch in Me that does not bear fruit He takes away; and every branch that bears fruit He prunes, that it may bear more fruit.

3 You are already clean because of the word which I have spoken to you.

4 Abide in Me, and I in you. As the branch cannot bear fruit of itself, unless it abides in the vine, neither can you, unless you abide in Me.

5 "I am the vine, you are the branches. He who abides in Me, and I in him, bears much fruit; for without Me you can do nothing.

6   *If anyone does not abide in Me, he is cast out as a branch and is withered; and they gather them and throw them into the fire, and they are burned.*

7   *If you abide in Me, and My words abide in you, you will ask what you desire, and it shall be done for you.*

8   *By this My Father is glorified, that you bear much fruit; so you will be My disciples.*

9   *"As the Father loved Me, I also have loved you; abide in My love.*

10   *If you keep My commandments, you will abide in My love, just as I have kept My Father's commandments and abide in His love.*

11   *"These things I have spoken to you, that My joy may remain in you, and that your joy may be full.*

12   *This is My commandment, that you love one another as I have loved you.*

13   *Greater love has no one than this, than to lay down one's life for his friends.*

14   *You are My friends if you do whatever I command you.*

15   *No longer do I call you servants, for a servant does not know what his master is doing; but I have called you friends, for all things that I heard from My Father I have made known to you.*

16   *You did not choose Me, but I chose you and appointed you that you should go and bear fruit, and that your fruit should remain, that whatever you ask the Father in My name He may give you.*

17   *These things I command you, that you love one another.*

18   *"If the world hates you, you know that it hated Me before it hated you.*

19   *If you were of the world, the world would love its own. Yet because you are not of the world, but I chose you out of the world, therefore the world hates you.*

20   *Remember the word that I said to you, 'A servant is not greater than his master.' If they persecuted Me, they will also persecute you. If they kept My word, they will keep yours also.*

abide in My love (v. 9)—not a mystical or emotional affection, but defined in verse 10 as obedience

your joy may be full (v. 11)—Obedient believers will experience the joy of the Lord.

Greater love . . . lay down one's life (v. 13)—Christians are called to exemplify the same kind of sacrificial giving toward one another, even if such sacrifice involves the laying down of one's life in imitation of Christ.

friends (vv. 14–15)—Those who follow Christ are privileged to be labeled as "friends" of God.

I chose you (v. 16)—All spiritual privileges are derived by virtue of God's sovereign choice, not human merit.

they would have no sin (v. 22)—does not mean that if Christ had not come, they would have been sinless, but that His coming incited within them the severest and most deadly sin of rejection and rebellion against the truth of God

These things (16:1)—the sobering words of 15:18–25

stumble (v. 1)—the idea is of setting a trap; the world would seek to trap and destroy the disciples

none of you asks (v. 5)—apparently the disciples were too absorbed in their own sorrow and worried about what would happen to them

when He has come (v. 8)—The coming of the Spirit at Pentecost was only about forty days away at this point.

convict (v. 8)—can have a judicial meaning in the sense of finding guilty and sentencing or convincing of one's true guilty state; the second meaning is probably best here

21 *But all these things they will do to you for My name's sake, because they do not know Him who sent Me.*

22 *If I had not come and spoken to them, they would have no sin, but now they have no excuse for their sin.*

23 *He who hates Me hates My Father also.*

24 *If I had not done among them the works which no one else did, they would have no sin; but now they have seen and also hated both Me and My Father.*

25 *But this happened that the word might be fulfilled which is written in their law, 'They hated Me without a cause.'*

26 *"But when the Helper comes, whom I shall send to you from the Father, the Spirit of truth who proceeds from the Father, He will testify of Me.*

27 *And you also will bear witness, because you have been with Me from the beginning.*

16:1 *"These things I have spoken to you, that you should not be made to stumble.*

2 *They will put you out of the synagogues; yes, the time is coming that whoever kills you will think that he offers God service.*

3 *And these things they will do to you because they have not known the Father nor Me.*

4 *But these things I have told you, that when the time comes, you may remember that I told you of them. "And these things I did not say to you at the beginning, because I was with you.*

5 *"But now I go away to Him who sent Me, and none of you asks Me, 'Where are You going?'*

6 *But because I have said these things to you, sorrow has filled your heart.*

7 *Nevertheless I tell you the truth. It is to your advantage that I go away; for if I do not go away, the Helper will not come to you; but if I depart, I will send Him to you.*

8 *And when He has come, He will convict the world of sin, and of righteousness, and of judgment:*

9 *of sin, because they do not believe in Me;*

10 *of righteousness, because I go to My Father and you see Me no more;*

11 *of judgment, because the ruler of this world is judged.*

12 *"I still have many things to say to you, but you cannot bear them now.*

13 *However, when He, the Spirit of truth, has come, He will guide you into all truth; for He will not speak on His own authority, but whatever He hears He will speak; and He will tell you things to come.*

14 *He will glorify Me, for He will take of what is Mine and declare it to you.*

15 *All things that the Father has are Mine. Therefore I said that He will take of Mine and declare it to you.*

16 *"A little while, and you will not see Me; and again a little while, and you will see Me, because I go to the Father."*

17 *Then some of His disciples said among themselves, "What is this that He says to us, 'A little while, and you will not see Me; and again a little while, and you will see Me'; and, 'because I go to the Father'?"*

18 *They said therefore, "What is this that He says, 'A little while'? We do not know what He is saying."*

19 *Now Jesus knew that they desired to ask Him, and He said to them, "Are you inquiring among yourselves about what I said, 'A little while, and you will not see Me; and again a little while, and you will see Me'?*

20 *Most assuredly, I say to you that you will weep and lament, but the world will rejoice; and you will be sorrowful, but your sorrow will be turned into joy.*

21 *A woman, when she is in labor, has sorrow because her hour has come; but as soon as she has given birth to the child, she no longer remembers the anguish, for joy that a human being has been born into the world.*

22 *Therefore you now have sorrow; but I will see you again and your heart will rejoice, and your joy no one will take from you.*

sin (v. 9)—probably the specific sin of not believing in Jesus as Messiah

righteousness (v. 10)—The Spirit shatters the pretensions of self-righteousness and exposes the dark recesses of the heart.

judgment (v. 11)—Since the world is under Satan's delusion, its judgments are faulty and evil, so the Spirit convinces men that their assessments of Christ and Satan are erroneous.

sorrow will be turned into joy (v. 20)—The very event that made the hate-filled world rejoice (that is, the killing of Christ) will be the same event that will lead to the world's sorrow and the believers' joy.

in that day (v. 23)—a reference to Pentecost

joy may be full (v. 24)—Here joy is related to answered prayer and a full supply of heavenly blessing.

in figurative language (v. 25)— The word means "veiled," an obscure statement pregnant with meaning; what was hard for the disciples to understand during the life of Christ would become clear following His resurrection and the coming of the Spirit.

overcome (v. 33)—The fundamental ground for endurance in persecution is the victory of Jesus over the world.

as many as You have given Him (17:2)—a reference to God's choosing of those who will come to Christ

23 "And in that day you will ask Me nothing. Most assuredly, I say to you, whatever you ask the Father in My name He will give you.

24 Until now you have asked nothing in My name. Ask, and you will receive, that your joy may be full.

25 "These things I have spoken to you in figurative language; but the time is coming when I will no longer speak to you in figurative language, but I will tell you plainly about the Father.

26 In that day you will ask in My name, and I do not say to you that I shall pray the Father for you;

27 for the Father Himself loves you, because you have loved Me, and have believed that I came forth from God.

28 I came forth from the Father and have come into the world. Again, I leave the world and go to the Father."

29 His disciples said to Him, "See, now You are speaking plainly, and using no figure of speech!

30 Now we are sure that You know all things, and have no need that anyone should question You. By this we believe that You came forth from God."

31 Jesus answered them, "Do you now believe?

32 Indeed the hour is coming, yes, has now come, that you will be scattered, each to his own, and will leave Me alone. And yet I am not alone, because the Father is with Me.

33 These things I have spoken to you, that in Me you may have peace. In the world you will have tribulation; but be of good cheer, I have overcome the world."

17:1 Jesus spoke these words, lifted up His eyes to heaven, and said: "Father, the hour has come. Glorify Your Son, that Your Son also may glorify You,

2 as You have given Him authority over all flesh, that He should give eternal life to as many as You have given Him.

3 And this is eternal life, that they may know You, the only true God, and Jesus Christ whom You have sent.

4   *I have glorified You on the earth. I have finished the work which You have given Me to do.*

5   *And now, O Father, glorify Me together with Yourself, with the glory which I had with You before the world was.*

6   *"I have manifested Your name to the men whom You have given Me out of the world. They were Yours, You gave them to Me, and they have kept Your word.*

7   *Now they have known that all things which You have given Me are from You.*

8   *For I have given to them the words which You have given Me; and they have received them, and have known surely that I came forth from You; and they have believed that You sent Me.*

9   *"I pray for them. I do not pray for the world but for those whom You have given Me, for they are Yours.*

10 *And all Mine are Yours, and Yours are Mine, and I am glorified in them.*

11 *Now I am no longer in the world, but these are in the world, and I come to You. Holy Father, keep through Your name those whom You have given Me, that they may be one as We are.*

12 *While I was with them in the world, I kept them in Your name. Those whom You gave Me I have kept; and none of them is lost except the son of perdition, that the Scripture might be fulfilled.*

13 *But now I come to You, and these things I speak in the world, that they may have My joy fulfilled in themselves.*

14 *I have given them Your word; and the world has hated them because they are not of the world, just as I am not of the world.*

15 *I do not pray that You should take them out of the world, but that You should keep them from the evil one.*

16 *They are not of the world, just as I am not of the world.*

17 *Sanctify them by Your truth. Your word is truth.*

They were Yours (v. 6)—a potent assertion that even before conversion, the yet-to-be-redeemed belong to God because of His election of them before the foundation of the world

I am no longer in the world (v. 11)—Jesus treated His departure as an already accomplished fact.

I kept them in your name (v. 12)—Jesus had protected His followers and had kept them safe.

son of perdition (v. 12)—a reference to Judas's destiny, that is, eternal damnation

Sanctify (v. 17)—to set apart for a particular use; believers are set apart for God and His purposes, so that they do only what God wants and they hate what He hates

the glory which You gave Me (v. 22)—The believer participates in all of the attributes and essence of God through the indwelling Holy Spirit.

18 As You sent Me into the world, I also have sent them into the world.

19 And for their sakes I sanctify Myself, that they also may be sanctified by the truth.

20 "I do not pray for these alone, but also for those who will believe in Me through their word;

21 that they all may be one, as You, Father, are in Me, and I in You; that they also may be one in Us, that the world may believe that You sent Me.

22 And the glory which You gave Me I have given them, that they may be one just as We are one:

23 I in them, and You in Me; that they may be made perfect in one, and that the world may know that You have sent Me, and have loved them as You have loved Me.

be with Me (v. 24)—this will be in heaven, where one can see the full glory that is Christ's

24 "Father, I desire that they also whom You gave Me may be with Me where I am, that they may behold My glory which You have given Me; for You loved Me before the foundation of the world.

25 O righteous Father! The world has not known You, but I have known You; and these have known that You sent Me.

26 And I have declared to them Your name, and will declare it, that the love with which You loved Me may be in them, and I in them."

1) In your own words, summarize the main ideas of what Christ taught in His metaphor of the vine and branches.

_____

_____

_____

2) What sobering words about the world's treatment of Christians did Jesus give His followers? Have you ever experienced this? What happened?

_____

_____

_____

3) What revelation about the Holy Spirit did Jesus give His disciples in the upper room? Why would these statements have been reassuring?

_____

_____

_____

GOING DEEPER

Jesus knew He would soon face suffering, yet He understood that nothing could separate Him from God's love and purpose. Read Romans 8:28–39 for insight into God's love.

EXPLORING THE MEANING

4) How does Paul's grand statement of ultimate love and eternal security in Christ echo our Lord's words in John 15–17?

_____

_____

_____

5) Jesus called His disciples "friends" (15:14–15). What does this mean to you? Why is it significant?

_____

_____

_____

6) What does the true "Lord's Prayer" (chapter 17) reveal about Jesus' goals and desires for His followers?

_____

_____

_____

Truth for Today

Christ prayed, "And this is eternal life, that they may know You, the only true God, and Jesus Christ whom You have sent. I have glorified You on the earth. I have finished the work which You have given Me to do" (17:3–4 NKJV). In His incarnation, Jesus glorified the Father by accomplishing His mission of providing eternal life to those who trust in Him, by reconciling lost men to the God they had forsaken. Jesus' supreme purpose on earth was "to seek and to save that which was lost" (Luke 19:10 NKJV). That is therefore also the supreme mission of Christ's church. The work of the church is an extension of the work of her Lord. "As You sent Me into the world, I also have sent them into the world" (17:18 NKJV).

Reflecting on the Text

7) What does it mean to you to be "sent" into the world? How does Christ's call translate into your daily life?

_____

_____

_____

_____

8) What "fruit" has been most evident in your Christian experience over the last six months? Why? On what area(s) of growth do you need to focus?

_____

_____

_____

_____

(Verses to consider: Gal. 5:19–23; Phil. 3:12–14; Heb. 13:15–16)

9) What is your specific part this week in "keeping [away] from the evil one" (17:15)? What practical precautions can you take to avoid temptation and stumbling into sin?

_____

_____

_____

Personal Response

Write out additional reflections, questions you may have, or a prayer.

ADDITIONAL NOTES

11

EXECUTION OF THE SON OF GOD

DRAWING NEAR

What situation in your life causes you to become timid or embarrassed about your faith in Christ? Why?

_____

_____

_____

As you read about Jesus' final hours, give thanks for His great sacrificial love.

THE CONTEXT

The events of Jesus' arrest, trial, and execution receive attention in chapters 18–19. Because John's purpose was to present Jesus as the Messiah and Son of God, he produced evidence to substantiate this purpose throughout his account of Jesus' passion. Through all the debasing, shameful acts that were directed toward Jesus, John skillfully shows that rather than detracting from His person and mission, these events actually constitute decisive evidence confirming who Jesus is and the reason for which Jesus had come.

John's account is very orderly and follows the logical flow of events: His rejection, His four trials, and His crucifixion. As you read about Jesus' final hours, give thanks for His sacrificial love.

KEYS TO THE TEXT

Crucifixion: The method of torture and execution used by the Romans to put Christ to death. At a crucifixion the victim usually was nailed or tied to a wooden stake and left to die. Crucifixion was used by many nations of the ancient world, including Assyria, Media, and Persia. Alexander the Great of Greece crucified 2,000 inhabitants of Tyre when he captured the city. The Romans later adopted this method and used it often throughout their empire. Crucifixion was the Romans' most severe form of execution, so it was reserved only for slaves and criminals. No Roman citizen could be crucified. (*Nelson's New Illustrated Bible Dictionary*)

Redeemed: The word *redeemed* is from a Greek word that was commonly used for buying a slave's freedom. Christ justifies those who believe in Him by buying them back from their slavery to sin. The price He paid was the only one high enough to redeem all of mankind, the "precious blood, as of a lamb unblemished and spotless, the blood of Christ" (1 Pet. 1:19 NKJV). We are all sinners. And either we pay the penalty for our own sin, which is eternal death, or we accept Jesus Christ's payment for it in sacrificing Himself, for which we receive eternal life. If the desire of our heart is to receive Him as Savior, to believe in and to accept His sacrifice, our sins are washed away at that point. The Bible says that without the shedding of blood there is no forgiveness for sin (Heb. 9:22) and that "the blood of Jesus His Son cleanses us from all sin" (1 John 1:7 NKJV). Jesus came as the perfect Sacrifice. The man whose sins are forgiven has them forgiven only because of Jesus Christ. But the blood of Jesus Christ will never be applied to us unless by faith we receive Him into our lives.

UNLEASHING THE TEXT

Read 18:1–19:37, noting the key words and definitions next to the passage.

John 18:1–19:37 (NKJV)

a garden (v. 1)—Gethsemane, an olive grove the name of which means "oil press"

entered (v. 1)—suggests a walled enclosure

a detachment of troops (v. 3)— a Roman cohort of anywhere from two hundred to one thousand men; these soldiers stayed at the Antonia Fortress near the temple complex to maintain security and order during Jewish feasts

Whom are you seeking? (vv. 4, 7)—By asking the question twice, Jesus was forcing His enemies to acknowledge they had no authority to take His disciples.

1 When Jesus had spoken these words, He went out with His disciples over the Brook Kidron, where there was a garden, which He and His disciples entered.

2 And Judas, who betrayed Him, also knew the place; for Jesus often met there with His disciples.

3 Then Judas, having received a detachment of troops, and officers from the chief priests and Pharisees, came there with lanterns, torches, and weapons.

4 Jesus therefore, knowing all things that would come upon Him, went forward and said to them, "Whom are you seeking?"

5 They answered Him, "Jesus of Nazareth." Jesus said to them, "I am He." And Judas, who betrayed Him, also stood with them.

6 Now when He said to them, "I am He," they drew back and fell to the ground.

7 Then He asked them again, "Whom are you seeking?" And they said, "Jesus of Nazareth."

8 Jesus answered, "I have told you that I am He. Therefore, if you seek Me, let these go their way,"

9   *that the saying might be fulfilled which He spoke,*
"Of those whom You gave Me I have lost none."

10   *Then Simon Peter, having a sword, drew it and*
struck the high priest's servant, and cut off his right
ear. The servant's name was Malchus.

11   *So Jesus said to Peter, "Put your sword into the*
sheath. Shall I not drink the cup which My Father
has given Me?"

12   *Then the detachment of troops and the captain and*
the officers of the Jews arrested Jesus and bound Him.

13   *And they led Him away to Annas first, for he was*
the father-in-law of Caiaphas who was high priest
that year.

14   *Now it was Caiaphas who advised the Jews that*
it was expedient that one man should die for the
people.

15   *And Simon Peter followed Jesus, and so did another*
disciple. Now that disciple was known to the high
priest, and went with Jesus into the courtyard of the
high priest.

16   *But Peter stood at the door outside. Then the other*
disciple, who was known to the high priest, went out
and spoke to her who kept the door, and brought
Peter in.

17   *Then the servant girl who kept the door said to*
Peter, "You are not also one of this Man's disciples,
are you?" He said, "I am not."

18   *Now the servants and officers who had made a*
fire of coals stood there, for it was cold, and they
warmed themselves. And Peter stood with them and
warmed himself.

19   *The high priest then asked Jesus about His disciples*
and His doctrine.

20   *Jesus answered him, "I spoke openly to the world.*
I always taught in synagogues and in the temple,
where the Jews always meet, and in secret I have
said nothing.

21   *Why do you ask Me? Ask those who have heard Me*
what I said to them. Indeed they know what I said."

I have lost none (v. 9)—None of Jesus' followers were arrested.

I not drink the cup (v. 11)—In the Old Testament, the "cup" is associated with suffering, wrath, and judgment.

Annas first (v. 13)—Annas was only High Priest from AD 6 to 15, but even after he was removed from office, he wielded tremendous influence over Caiaphas, his son-in-law.

Caiaphas (v. 13)—John does not record this examination in more detail; see Matthew 26:57–58.

known to the high priest (v. 16)—The word "known" can imply friendship; John was more than just an acquaintance.

Praetorium (v. 28)—the head-quarters of the commanding officer of the Roman military or military governor (that is, Pilate)

lest they should be defiled (v. 28)—Because of their oral tradition, the Jewish leaders believed they might become morally polluted by entering the residence of a Gentile (never mind the evil they were committing against the Son of God!).

It is not lawful (v. 31)—Rome had taken from the Jews the power and right of capital punishment.

22 *And when He had said these things, one of the officers who stood by struck Jesus with the palm of his hand, saying, "Do You answer the high priest like that?"*

23 *Jesus answered him, "If I have spoken evil, bear witness of the evil; but if well, why do you strike Me?"*

24 *Then Annas sent Him bound to Caiaphas the high priest.*

25 *Now Simon Peter stood and warmed himself. Therefore they said to him, "You are not also one of His disciples, are you?" He denied it and said, "I am not!"*

26 *One of the servants of the high priest, a relative of him whose ear Peter cut off, said, "Did I not see you in the garden with Him?"*

27 *Peter then denied again; and immediately a rooster crowed.*

28 *Then they led Jesus from Caiaphas to the Praetorium, and it was early morning. But they themselves did not go into the Praetorium, lest they should be defiled, but that they might eat the Passover.*

29 *Pilate then went out to them and said, "What accusation do you bring against this Man?"*

30 *They answered and said to him, "If He were not an evildoer, we would not have delivered Him up to you."*

31 *Then Pilate said to them, "You take Him and judge Him according to your law." Therefore the Jews said to him, "It is not lawful for us to put anyone to death,"*

32 *that the saying of Jesus might be fulfilled which He spoke, signifying by what death He would die.*

33 *Then Pilate entered the Praetorium again, called Jesus, and said to Him, "Are You the King of the Jews?"*

34 *Jesus answered him, "Are you speaking for yourself about this, or did others tell you this concerning Me?"*

35 *Pilate answered, "Am I a Jew? Your own nation and the chief priests have delivered You to me. What have You done?"*

36 *Jesus answered, "My kingdom is not of this world. If My kingdom were of this world, My servants would fight, so that I should not be delivered to the Jews; but now My kingdom is not from here."*

37 *Pilate therefore said to Him, "Are You a king then?" Jesus answered, "You say rightly that I am a king. For this cause I was born, and for this cause I have come into the world, that I should bear witness to the truth. Everyone who is of the truth hears My voice."*

38 *Pilate said to Him, "What is truth?" And when he had said this, he went out again to the Jews, and said to them, "I find no fault in Him at all.*

39 *"But you have a custom that I should release someone to you at the Passover. Do you therefore want me to release to you the King of the Jews?"*

40 *Then they all cried again, saying, "Not this Man, but Barabbas!" Now Barabbas was a robber.*

19:1 *So then Pilate took Jesus and scourged Him.*

2 *And the soldiers twisted a crown of thorns and put it on His head, and they put on Him a purple robe.*

3 *Then they said, "Hail, King of the Jews!" And they struck Him with their hands.*

4 *Pilate then went out again, and said to them, "Behold, I am bringing Him out to you, that you may know that I find no fault in Him."*

5 *Then Jesus came out, wearing the crown of thorns and the purple robe. And Pilate said to them, "Behold the Man!"*

6 *Therefore, when the chief priests and officers saw Him, they cried out, saying, "Crucify Him, crucify Him!" Pilate said to them, "You take Him and crucify Him, for I find no fault in Him."*

7 *The Jews answered him, "We have a law, and according to our law He ought to die, because He made Himself the Son of God."*

8 *Therefore, when Pilate heard that saying, he was the more afraid,*

9 *and went again into the Praetorium, and said to Jesus, "Where are You from?" But Jesus gave him no answer.*

My kingdom is not of this world (v. 36)—Jesus meant that His kingdom is not connected to earthly, political, and national entities, nor does it have its origin in this evil world system that is in rebellion against God.

Now Barabbas was a robber (v. 40)—Mark 15:7 indicates that Barabbas was also a kind of guerrilla terrorist.

scourged (19:1)—flogged with a multi-thonged whip embedded with pieces of bone or metal; this inhuman punishment left its victims maimed, their bones, veins, and muscles exposed

purple robe (v. 2)—an attempt to mock Jesus' claims to be the King of the Jews

Behold the Man! (v. 5)—a sarcastic announcement by Pilate, perhaps meaning, "This poor, pathetic, bloodied soul—this is the One you fear so much?"

"Where are You from?" (v. 9)—As a superstitious Roman, Pilate was fearful when he pondered Christ's origins.

the one who delivered Me to you has the greater sin (v. 11)—a reference either to Judas or Caiaphas

the judgment seat (v. 13)—the official site of Roman legal pronouncements; Pilate agreed to rule on the original charge of sedition

bearing His cross (v. 17)—the cross-beam or horizontal bar only

Golgotha (v. 17)—an English transliteration of the Greek which, in turn, is a translation of the Aramaic word meaning "skull"; the hill of crucifixion probably resembled a human skull

wrote a title (v. 19)—customary in executions to specify the victims' crimes; here Pilate intended to mock the Jews by giving Christ the title they so hated

10 Then Pilate said to Him, "Are You not speaking to me? Do You not know that I have power to crucify You, and power to release You?"

11 Jesus answered, "You could have no power at all against Me unless it had been given you from above. Therefore the one who delivered Me to you has the greater sin."

12 From then on Pilate sought to release Him, but the Jews cried out, saying, "If you let this Man go, you are not Caesar's friend. Whoever makes himself a king speaks against Caesar."

13 When Pilate therefore heard that saying, he brought Jesus out and sat down in the judgment seat in a place that is called The Pavement, but in Hebrew, Gabbatha.

14 Now it was the Preparation Day of the Passover, and about the sixth hour. And he said to the Jews, "Behold your King!"

15 But they cried out, "Away with Him, away with Him! Crucify Him!" Pilate said to them, "Shall I crucify your King?" The chief priests answered, "We have no king but Caesar!"

16 Then he delivered Him to them to be crucified. Then they took Jesus and led Him away.

17 And He, bearing His cross, went out to a place called the Place of a Skull, which is called in Hebrew, Golgotha,

18 where they crucified Him, and two others with Him, one on either side, and Jesus in the center.

19 Now Pilate wrote a title and put it on the cross. And the writing was: JESUS OF NAZARETH, THE KING OF THE JEWS.

20 Then many of the Jews read this title, for the place where Jesus was crucified was near the city; and it was written in Hebrew, Greek, and Latin.

21 Therefore the chief priests of the Jews said to Pilate, "Do not write, 'The King of the Jews,' but, 'He said, "I am the King of the Jews." ' "

22 Pilate answered, "What I have written, I have written."

23 *Then the soldiers, when they had crucified Jesus, took His garments and made four parts, to each soldier a part, and also the tunic. Now the tunic was without seam, woven from the top in one piece.*

24 *They said therefore among themselves, "Let us not tear it, but cast lots for it, whose it shall be," that the Scripture might be fulfilled which says: "They divided My garments among them, And for My clothing they cast lots." Therefore the soldiers did these things.*

25 *Now there stood by the cross of Jesus His mother, and His mother's sister, Mary the wife of Clopas, and Mary Magdalene.*

26 *When Jesus therefore saw His mother, and the disciple whom He loved standing by, He said to His mother, "Woman, behold your son!"*

27 *Then He said to the disciple, "Behold your mother!" And from that hour that disciple took her to his own home.*

28 *After this, Jesus, knowing that all things were now accomplished, that the Scripture might be fulfilled, said, "I thirst!"*

29 *Now a vessel full of sour wine was sitting there; and they filled a sponge with sour wine, put it on hyssop, and put it to His mouth.*

30 *So when Jesus had received the sour wine, He said, "It is finished!" And bowing His head, He gave up His spirit.*

31 *Therefore, because it was the Preparation Day, that the bodies should not remain on the cross on the Sabbath (for that Sabbath was a high day), the Jews asked Pilate that their legs might be broken, and that they might be taken away.*

32 *Then the soldiers came and broke the legs of the first and of the other who was crucified with Him.*

33 *But when they came to Jesus and saw that He was already dead, they did not break His legs.*

34 *But one of the soldiers pierced His side with a spear, and immediately blood and water came out.*

sour wine (v. 29)—The purpose of this drink (unlike the pain-killing wine offered Christ on His way to the cross) was to prolong life and increase the torture and pain.

"It is finished!" (v. 30)—a triumphant cry indicating "mission accomplished"; the single Greek word used here by John has also been found in extra-biblical literature on a tax receipt and there has the meaning "paid in full"

their legs might be broken (v. 31)—to hasten death by preventing the victim from lifting himself so as to catch a breath

35 *And he who has seen has testified, and his testimony is true; and he knows that he is telling the truth, so that you may believe.*

36 *For these things were done that the Scripture should be fulfilled, "Not one of His bones shall be broken."*

37 *And again another Scripture says, "They shall look on Him whom they pierced."*

1) How did Christ demonstrate His deity at the time of His arrest in the Garden? Why did these acts only intensify the guilt of Jesus' enemies?

_____

_____

_____

_____

_____

(Verse to consider: Luke 22:51)

2) Compare Peter's response in the Garden with his response at Jesus' trial. Why do you think there was such a change? (See 18:10–27)

_____

_____

_____

_____

3) Based on John's account, how would you describe Pilate? What kind of man was he? What was his opinion of Christ?

_____

_____

_____

_____

GOING DEEPER

Jesus' life and death were foretold in the Old Testament. Read Psalm 22:1–21 for one prophecy.